The Alodia Scrapbook

Vol. 1: Creating a New Paradigm, 2000-03

HENRY GEORGE INSTITUTE

The Alodia Scrapbook

Vol. 1: Creating a New Paradigm, 2000-03

Produced, edited and designed by Lindy Davies

ISBN 978-0-9741844-2-5

Library of Congress Control Number: 2010913436

Copyright © 2010 by the Henry George Institute
121 East 30th Street
New York, NY 10016
www.henrygeorge.org

All rights reserved.

Welcome to Alodia

Early in 2001, an offshoot to the Henry George Institute's website appeared, greeting the visitor with these words:

> *Alodia is a struggling, debt-saddled, former French colony in West Africa. Its agriculture and industry function well below their capacity; it has a large and growing population of AIDS victims; it has deepened its people's suffering in order to secure debt relief; its natural environment has been deeply degraded. However, Alodia differs in one significant respect from all the other nations in such straits: it is fictional.*

The site invited people to read about Alodia's history, its vital statistics and its new departure — and then to take part in the shaping of a nation's history, by telling, through posts on online message boards, what would happen next.

As things got going, it became evident that there weren't so terribly many people who had the kind of free time that our project asked them to devote. Lots of people thought the project was a good idea and promised to stop by; few, alas, stayed around long enough to become part of the citizenry.

We did find some loyal Alodians, though. I want to deeply thank the team of Sunny Akuopha, Jonathan Hall and Kleo Pullin, who wrote, with me, the material that is collected herein. Now, it has been a few years since we worked together on this project, and I apologize if my retelling of the story has pulled their characters in directions their creators didn't intend.

For their invaluable help with this project, I also want to thank Mike Curtis, Hanno Beck, Sonny Rivera, Cay Hehner, and — last but certainly not least — Alodia Arnold, for letting us name the country after her.

— *Lindy Davies*, September 2010

Alodia's "Sleight-of-Hand" Coup

The Political Economist. **Aloville, 7 January 2001**

Last week's takeover of the Government of Alodia by its Army caught the world by surprise. Even the two announcements that were broadcast prior to the televised speech by General Samuel Akuopha on New Year's Day, displayed the nation's seal and flag and said merely that "An historic event will occur at 1:00 PM this afternoon."

While the regime of President Jacques Oshodi, who was re-elected to a third four-year term in 1998, was widely unpopular, it was considered by most observers to be stable. Alodia has suffered from the now all-too familiar litany of African problems, but it appeared to be making progress at restoring solvency through debt restructuring, and its agricultural sector and tourism industry had both been posting gains. Negotiations for debt relief under the International Monetary Fund's "Heavily Indebted Poor Nations" initiative have been proceeding, and some of Alodia's debt appeared destined to be forgiven.

Samuel Akuopha

What many foreign observers, and indeed many Alodian citizens, seem not to have been aware of, however, is the stature of the Army in this nation. Courted at various times in its history by both the United States and the Soviet Union, it was well-provisioned with military hardware. The country has long maintained an all-volunteer army, and military careers are generally viewed as prestigious and desirable. There is also, evidently, no lack of discipline or organization. When troops moved in the Capital on this New Year's Day, their operations were almost completely simultaneous. Some 150 heavily armed soldiers materialized at the National Assembly at 1:00 PM, immediately disarming the security forces on hand. They proceeded to evacuate and shut the building in less than two hours' time; no shots were fired and no injuries reported. The seizing of executive offices and other key government departments were similarly swift. The army appears to have been ordered against making any statements at all. Aside from General Akuopha himself, no reports of any statements made by any Alodian soldier have yet surfaced in the press.

Akuopha's speech harkened repeatedly to the memory of Alodia's "founding President," the much-loved Jean-Henri Alo, whom Akuopha claimed as personal friend and mentor. The speech emphasized, albeit vaguely, reform of economic and taxation policy. Its most striking element, however, was the assertion that Alodia would unilaterally cease making payments on its external debt. Alodia's debts are considerable, with total foreign obligations of some $25 billion, and it has been meeting revenue shortfalls with new borrowing and other aid of nearly $1 billion per year.

International reaction to Akuopha's debt-policy gauntlet has been largely dismissive. A senior White House official repeated the US's official condemnation of the coup, adding that "on the international debt policy, I don't think he has thought that one through very well." IMF spokesman Harvey Rugla laid out, in a press conference, the world financial community's probable response to Alodia's promised repudiation — which would include the severest economic sanctions available under the IMF guidelines. Rugla stressed that Alodia was a member nation and "knows the rules as well as anybody." But, he added, such a drastic outcome was unlikely. "It would be a policy of economic suicide, and they have enough problems as it is. We expect this repudiation plan to be dropped in very short order."

Alodian sources, however, seem convinced that the new

regime will be sticking with its position. Akuopha himself has given one press conference since the coup, in which he stated, "The banks are portraying me as not having done my homework. But this plan did not, after all, just occur to us this week. We have been studying it for quite some time, and we will implement it with firm deliberation. We have the team of experts we need to make it work."

As for Alodians themselves, many have expressed relief that the Oshodi regime has been ousted, even if they have reservations about the way it was done. There does appear to be considerable confusion about Akuopha's economic proposals. Senator after Senator from the now-disbanded National Assembly has appeared in the press calling for specifics on just what it is that Akuopha plans to do. Akuopha, who has installed his staff in the Presidential Palace and is using the residence as an office, has promised to publish his economic plan in detail by the end of this month. All those with their eyes on the new President, foreign leaders, international banks, and his own citizens, seem inclined to give Akuopha that much time — if not, perhaps, much more.

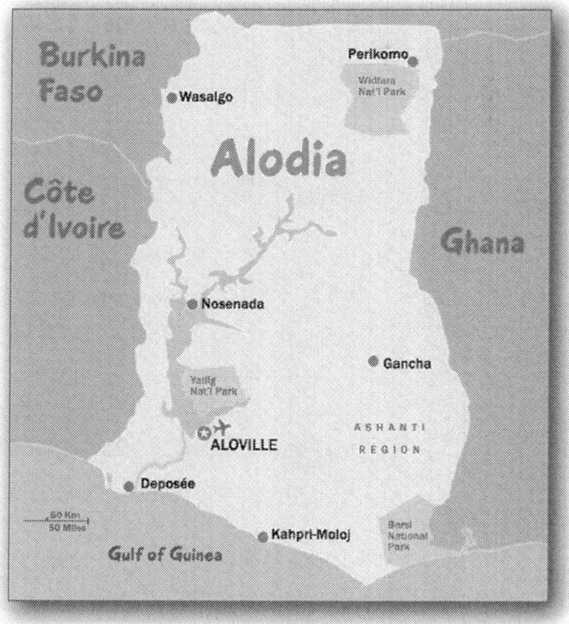

Speech of General Samuel Akuopha to the People of Alodia

Aloville, 1 January 2001

My greetings to you all, my greatest wishes for peace and hope to you, on this occasion that is momentous, but not joyous. I will refrain from the kind of chest-beating banter that often characterizes a speech like this: I will not talk down to you. Our society is in stark and desperate crisis. We are — today — in the very gravest danger of losing our community, our children's future, our hopes for greater things. We are in danger of becoming a region of stunted thugs with no vision beyond the next meal — or the next round of ammunition.

How did we get here? I review the events of the last thirty-eight years in my mind, and I see the blunders, the corruptions, the fruitless alliances, the squandered wealth, the plain bad luck. On paper these things, perhaps, add up — but when I see the all-but endless shantytown that surrounds Aloville, when I see the thousands of orphaned children, it is almost more than my heart can bear, and I ask again: How did we get here? And I say: We must do better. We must, together, build a way out of this Hell.

Perhaps it is better that my friend and mentor, Jean-Henri Alo, left us early, when his beloved country was still floating on the pride of recent independence. How I still remember the bright challenge in his eyes as he spoke of a national campaign for vision, education and common sense — those most primary human values that have been so sorely lacking in our political discourse. "Our Alo" instilled in us a sense of optimism, a belief in our capacity to join, in equal status and dignity, the rest of the world's nations. He was a beloved, a visionary leader — but, alas: he was no economist.

But then — which is worse? For the last five years our government has been under the sway of economists, cold-eyed, calculating men without vision, without the slightest understanding of the realities of Alodia. Our poverty is certainly real. But so is our potential. Are we children? Are we a nation of mental incompetents? Our government has been inept, our people have been suffering — but we are not unable to stand. We do not need to borrow their money to buy the crutches that they offer to sell us.

Recently Alodia — like so many other benighted nations — has been seeking so-called "relief" through the plan offered by the International Monetary Fund on behalf of "Heavily Indebted Poor Countries," One of the requirements of this process is that a document be prepared, called a "Poverty Reduction Strategy Paper." And although we were instructed to undertake this exercise with the broadest possible input from concerned elements of our society — our working people, in other words, or those who cannot find work — how many of you have heard of it? How many of you were consulted? And no wonder. For the plan we were offered, to enable us to continue borrowing from Western banks, stipulated that the government must cut social spending by forty percent. This, at a time when one Alodian adult in ten suffers from AIDS, when schools and hospitals are both filled to bursting, when tourists in Kahpri-Moloj cannot count on electric or phone service. Poverty reduction, they call it. Poverty reduction! A "growth-friendly" strategy, so that we can borrow more Western money to service our Western debt, while our people cannot get medical care or clean water. The structural adjustment program that was practiced for over a decade now has paid no debts, just replaced them with bigger debts. It has robbed Alodians of their wealth. It is unjust, and it is killing us. We now choose another path.

There will be accusations of autocracy. We will be called a "military junta" that has seized control of a "democratically elected government." Most of our people fully well know the truth of these matters, but so that there is no confusion let me state some truths as clearly as I can. Today, the term "democracy" is most often a mere bauble used to prettify, and thus divert attention from, underlying corruption. The 1996 Presidential election, which was praised in the Western press, was won by Jacques Oshodi with 98.6% of the vote. A normal temperature, indeed. Is there such unanimity in favor of that government or its policies? The foreign observers only visited a few polling stations in the capitals and big cities, whereas a majority of Alodians live in rural areas where there were widespread irregularities. Many opposition leaders were detained and their supporters thrown into prison! To all these people, including all other political prisoners, I now grant general amnesty and order their immediate release.

This plan did not, after all, just occur to us this week. We have been studying it for quite some time, and we will implement it with firm deliberation.

There will be democracy in Alodia. There will be free and fair elections. First, however, our ground must be cultivated with the conditions of economic justice and prosperity that makes it possible for democracy to take root. For as a wise reformer, the American economist Henry George, wrote: "forms are nothing when the substance is gone, and the forms of popular government are those from which the substance of freedom may most easily go. Political equality, co-existing with an increasing tendency to the unequal distribution of wealth, must ultimately beget the despotism of organized tyranny or the worse despotism of anarchy." Alodia has experienced both.

We must prepare the ground. And so, while the political timetable that we offer you may be somewhat vague, our economic agenda is utterly specific.

The staggering sums, over twenty billion United States dollars, that were borrowed by this nation from Western lenders or from the so-called "Bretton Woods Institutions" were not loans contracted by the people of Alodia. The result of these loans has not been to benefit the people of Alodia but to impoverish them. Therefore our people — the only source of wealth that any nation can ever have — cannot justly be required to repay these loans. From this day forward Alodia will cease all service payments on outstanding foreign debt. For some years we have maintained a trade surplus; should that situation become reversed we would, of course, honor terms of credit arranged in the current year. But we shall not pay one more Franc on any Alodian debt undertaken before this year.

We are aware that this may bring repercussions. That cannot be our concern. We cannot speak for other nations. They must evaluate their own situations and take what actions they find advisable — but for Alodia, the time for prudence is gone. Our situation is desperate, and we must act.

It will be said, "Your country is a basket case — to deny it further emergency credit from the West will be suicidal!" But the policies we have pursued over the last decade were evidently more suicidal. Will we writhe, like junkies, once our supply of financial drug is cut off? No, fellow citizens of Alodia, I say to you today that we will not. We will stand. We will grow. We will build. We are not a nation of children. Neither our limbs nor our hearts are broken, not yet.

So that there is no confusion, let me state some truths as clearly as I can. The land, the natural resources and opportunities of a nation, are truly the property of that nation. If there is profit to be gained from the possession of the land, the natural resources of a nation, that profit must be used to build schools, roads, communication lines, and hospitals. Therefore I say to you that the full rental value of the land, the natural resources and opportunities of Alodia will be fully and fairly assessed, and will be collected for the public revenue of Alodia.

The wealth that an individual creates with his labor, his ingenuity, his industry and skill, is not the rightful property of any other man, and must not be confiscated. Therefore I say to you that all taxes on incomes, on commerce and sales, on transportation and exchange and imports will be fully and totally abolished in the Republic of Alodia.

The right of every person to keep in undisturbed possession his home, his crops, his improvements to the land, is fundamental to liberty and this right shall no longer be disrespected in the Republic of Alodia.

Our people share with the generations yet to be born, and even with the animals, that know no national boundaries, the right to unpoisoned air, water and soil. Therefore the Nation of Alodia declares its right and its intention to enact such regulations as it deems correct for the securing of these rights — regardless of any action, sanction or restriction adopted by any other nation or association of nations. The Republic of Alodia re-asserts its full, complete and unconditional sovereignty over its internationally recognized territory and all rights pertaining thereto. Other jurisdictions, other bodies must do as they see fit.

It is clear to me that I will not, when this day is through, have shed the labels of "military coup" and "strongman" that have been applied, and furthermore it is clear to me that what is said here today will be twisted, in bizarre ways, for months to come. So that there is no confusion, let me state some truths as clearly as I can. I have had a military career. I am a General in the Army of Alodia. As such I have, paradoxically, enjoyed a career that has probably been among the most peaceful in Africa. Our armed forces have been lavishly, lethally equipped by the great empires that vied for control of the world. We functioned as a deterrent; we put down the occasional demonstration, riot or unruly gang of refugees, but we have never been invaded; we have never fought a war. Indeed, we were ready to fight for independence in Alo's day, armed with only a tiny fraction of the firepower we now possess, but on the very eve, independence was granted by the French who were tired, by then, of fighting Africans.

I tell this story to underscore the simple point that Alodia's army is stable, its morale is high, and it is dug in for the long haul. The armed forces have maintained discipline as each regime has arrived in Aloville, and then departed. The army has ruthlessly kept itself well-fed while civilians were starving. Am I proud of that? No. But this I know: when a time comes such as now, when bold moves are required to ensure our very survival, the army of Alodia can be trusted to maintain the necessary order and to do what must be done.

The economic program on which we embark today is our only hope. But hope it is — radiant hope. Some will condemn us. Many will misrepresent and misunderstand us. But I say to you today, fellow citizens of Alodia, that if, together, we embark on an economic renaissance in the spirit of Jean-Henri Alo, with Vision, Education and Common Sense — if we do this, I say to you today that there is only one way that we can be thwarted. Only by the overwhelming force of an empire; only by utter destruction. But we will not be destroyed. Freed from thievery, given access to the land that is their birthright, the people of Alodia will realize their potential to build a beautiful, successful, just, prosperous, free, African nation.

Alodia Fact Sheet

excerpted from the *CIA World Factbook,* 2001

Background: Gained independence from France in 1961, under its first President, John Henry Alo, who died of cancer in 1965. Alo seemed to have been hand-picked for leadership by the departing colonial authorities, yet his "national vision" campaign for "education, self-reliance and common sense" was wildly popular among citizens. After his death the country, originally called "Limbotho," was renamed. The next eight years were spent under a US-supported anti-communist regime, which was overthrown in 1973 by an uprising that led to the adoption of a socialist government with strong ties to the Soviet Union, which supplied large stocks of weapons through the early 1980s. Heavy foreign debts were built up during both periods. Recently the army has seized control of the government, promising radical economic and taxation reforms.

Geography

Location: Western Africa, bordering the North Atlantic Ocean, between Ghana and Cote d'Ivoire

Area: 318,864 sq km — comparative: slightly larger than Nebraska

Border countries: Burkina Faso 584 km, Ghana 668 km, Cote d'Ivoire 716 km

Climate: tropical; warm and comparatively dry along southeast coast; hot and humid in southwest; hot and dry in north. Seasons: rainy season, late April to October; dry season, Nov. - March.

Terrain: mostly flat to undulating plains; large wetlands in the Jasil River delta; mountains in the central highlands

Lowest point: Gulf of Guinea 0 m
Highest point: Mont Furabi 1,662 m

Natural resources: titanium, tungsten, gems, manganese, cobalt, bauxite, copper

Land use:
arable land: 12%
permanent crops: 7%
permanent pastures: 30%
forests and woodland: 18%
other: 33% (1993 est.)

Irrigated land: 1,490 sq km (1993 est.)

Natural hazards: coast has heavy surf; during the rainy season the low-lying port of Deposée has frequent torrential flooding

Environment: current issues: deforestation; water pollution from sewage and industrial and agricultural effluents, leading to outbreaks of dangerously contaminated fish in Lake Banneker

People

Population: 22,480,910
note: estimates for this country explicitly take into account the effects of excess mortality due to AIDS; this can result in lower life expectancy, higher infant mortal-

ity and death rates, lower population and growth rates, and changes in the distribution of population by age and sex than would otherwise be expected (2000 est.)

Age structure:
0-14 years: 49.37% (male 3,726,388; female 3,696,462)
15-64 years: 48.36% (male 4,222,333; female 3,985,249)
65 years and over: 1.29% (male 175,606; female 174,912) (2000)

Population growth rate: 2.86% (2000)

Birth rate: 48.78 births/1,000 population (2000 est.)

Net migration rate: 1.6 migrant(s)/ 1,000 population (2000 est.)
note: after Liberia's civil war started in 1990, more than 350,000 refugees fled to Alodia; by the end of 1999 all Liberian refugees were assumed to have returned; the 2000 rate reflects labor in migration

Life expectancy at birth:
total population: 44.15 years
male: 42.72 years
female: 45.63 years (2000 est.)

Total fertility rate: 5.9 children born/ woman (2000 est.)

Ethnic groups: Baoule 23%, Bete 18%, Senoufou 15%, Malinke 11%, Agni, Africans from other countries (mostly Burkinabe and Malians, about 3 million), non-Africans 130,000 to 330,000 (French 30,000 and Pakistani 80,000 to 150,000)

Religions: Christian 50%, Muslim 26%, Indigenous 24% (some of these are also numbered among the Christians and Muslims)

Languages: French (official), 60 native dialects with Asante the most widely spoken

Literacy: (age 15 and over can read and write)
total population: 60.5%
male: 67%
female: 45%

Government

Capital: Aloville

Administrative divisions: 11 states, with populations (x1000); Perikomo 800, Nienemba 1750, Wasalgo 900, Widfara 1900, Tingi 2050, Nosenada 1800, Gancha 1950, Bangolo 2150, Brandy 1100, Deposée 2200, Kaphri-Moloj 2250, Aloville 3630

Independence: 26 March, 1961

Constitution: 4 June 1962; new constitution adopted October 1992

Legal system: based on French civil law system and customary law; has not accepted compulsory ICJ jurisdiction

Executive branch:
Chief of state: Gen. Samuel AKUOPHA (since 1 January 2001); note — took power following a military coup against the government of former President Jacques Butho OSHODI; president is both chief of state and head of government

Elections: prior to the coup, president elected by popular vote for a four-year term; election last held November 1996. Results of the last election prior to the coup were: Jacques Butho OSHODI elected president; percent of vote — Jacques Butho OSHODI 98.6%

Legislative branch: unicameral National Assembly or *Assemblee Nationale* (50 seats; members are elected by direct popular vote to serve six-year terms)

Judicial branch: Supreme Court *(Cour Supreme)*

Political parties and leaders: Alodian Worker's Party or PAT [Gali SEGUN]; Party of Liberty [Vincent AGUNABO]; Christian Coalition [Isabela DERYL-WALI]; various smaller parties

Diplomatic representation in the US: Samuel Confidence DOTSE; chancery: 3222 Massachusetts Avenue NW, Washington, DC 20007

Economy overview: Once among the world's largest producers and exporters of coffee, cocoa beans, and palm oil, Alodia's agricultural production has decreased sharply during the 1990s, due to a convergence of factors including frequent flooding, political instability and the AIDS crisis. The economy appears less precarious than it actually is, due to the popularity of aichacite, a blue-green gem, considerably harder than the emerald, which is found in only one place in the world: Alodia's central highlands. The Alodian economy has been lagging for several years since the collapse of the Soviet Union, which provided its main market for agricultural exports. Debt rescheduling by multilateral lenders and France has been slow to advance, due to the Oshodi regime's difficulty in imposing the mandated reforms. However, a refinancing plan adopted in 1998 under the HIPC initiative allowed for some infrastructure-repair projects, but widespread job losses and rising health care costs overshadowed their positive effects. The 50% devaluation of Franc Zone currencies on 12 January 1994 caused a one-time jump in the inflation rate to 26% in 1994; inflation nearly spun out of control in the following two years, subsiding only as economic output fell drastically in 1999. The Akuopha government's proposed reforms may destabilize international relationships, further threatening the domestic economy.

GDP: purchasing power parity - $22.7 billion (1999 est.)
GDP - per capita: purchasing power parity - $1,100 (1999 est.)

composition by sector:
agriculture: 40%
industry: 32%
services: 18%
civil service: 10% (1998)

Household income by percentage share:
lowest 10%: 2.1%
highest 10%: 31.5% (1988)

Inflation rate (consumer prices): 21.5% (1999 est.)

Unemployment rate: NA% (Note: Unemployment figures stated in recent documents have been widely deemed inaccurate, and the new regime has issued a statement placing the true rate at over 15%.)

Budget: revenues: $2.3 billion expenditures: $2.9 billion, including capital expenditures of $1.7 billion (1997 est.)

Industries: foodstuffs, beverages, tourism, wood products, fishing, textiles, fertilizer, construction materials, electricity

Exports: commodities: cocoa 37%, coffee, tropical woods, cotton, bananas, pineapples, palm oil, cotton, fish ($3.2 billion, 1998)

partners: France 17%, Russia 12%, Netherlands 9%, Italy 6% (1998)

Imports: commodities: food, consumer goods; capital goods, fuel, transport equipment ($2.6 billion, 1999 est.)

partners: France 29%, US 5%, Italy 5%, Germany 5% (1998)

External debt: $21.7 billion (1998 est.)

Currency: *Communaute Financiere Africaine* franc (CFAF)
note: since 1 January 1999, the CFAF is pegged to the euro at a rate of 655.957 CFA francs per euro

Communications

Telephone system: moderate by African standards, and operating well below capacity
Radio broadcast stations: AM 2, FM 8, shortwave 3 (1998)

Radios: 1.86 million (1997)

Televisions: 700,000 (1997)

Internet Service Providers: 1

Transportation

Railways:
total: 520 km

Highways: total: 45,400 km
paved: 4,100 km
unpaved: 41,300 km (1996 est.)

Waterways: 1,900 km navigable rivers, canals, and numerous coastal lagoons. Lake Banneker, one of the world's largest man-made lakes, provides 1,155 km of arterial and feeder waterways.

Airports - with paved runways: 6
over 3,047 m: 1

Military

Army: Army, with the following major branches: Air Force, paramilitary *Gendarmerie*, Republican Guard, *Sapeur-Pompier* (Military Fire Group)

Military manpower, fit for military service: males age 15-49: 1,952,882 (2000)

Military expenditures - dollar figure: $68 million (FY96)
note: Since the 1970s, the Alodian military has appeared to receive far greater funding than offical reports have indicated; there have been persistent allegations of underground financing schemes for military gear and operations.

Transnational Issues - Ilicit drugs: producer of cannabis, mostly for local consumption; transshipment point for Southwest and Southeast Asian heroin to Europe and occasionally to the US; domestic production and processing of cocaine for US and European markets is rumored.

A Brief Historical Sketch

The country formerly called "Limbotho" was one of the French colonies along West Africa's "Ivory Coast" which became independent in the early 1960s. Up to that point its history largely parallels that of other French African colonies such as Cote d'Ivoire, Senegal or Mali. But a distinctive item in the nation's early development is the nearly-universal acclaim and respect afforded to its first President, Jean-Henri Alo.

Educated in Paris, Alo was admitted to the French Bar in his mid-20s. He was also an accomplished musician, and became known in the dynamic Paris jazz scene of the 50s (and placed his idols, Miles Davis and John Coltrane, on Limbotho's early postage stamps). Politically, Alo was an individualist libertarian. In his speeches, which were often memorable, he stressed freedom and individual rights, and often quoted Thomas Paine. Alo also frequently returned to themes of self-reliance and common sense, and he was fond of quoting Benjamin Franklin, and Benjamin Banneker, a little-known African-American inventor of the early 19th century.

Alo believed in minimal government, and local control of social services and functions, to the greatest extent possible. In some areas, such as the notable refusal to legislate against such "victimless crimes" as prostitution or drug possession, Alo's libertarian influence survives to the present day. However, the nation's political system soon veered into a more conventional path.

Limbothans of all walks of life (the nation was re-named after Alo's death) displayed a remarkably potent sense of national pride and purpose in the nation's first three years of independence. This was largely due to the inspiration of the beloved Alo, but also to their good fortune in enjoying a relatively peaceful and orderly transition to independence. Limbotho's progress was often held up in the Western (particularly French) press of a shining example of the "new Africa." Much was accomplished by volunteerism in the nation's first three years: schools were built and modernized; local clinics and libraries were established. But, the glowing reports often had a "human interest" focus, and failed to note the growing strains in the Alo regime's attempt to run a modern nation as though it were a village. Shortages, unrest and occasional violence intensified as Alo's illness began to remove him from the day-to-day work of "administering his nation."

Jean-Henri Alo, inaugural portrait

After Alo's death of cancer in 1964, elections were held and his protege, Laurent Wodie, was elected President by a large majority. The regime capitalized on the huge popularity of its late founder and re-named the country. Because of its "libertarian" stance, the United States was friendly to Alodia, and advised it in many ways. Ironically, however, US influence manifested itself in such "socialistic" measures as a vastly increased central government, a reorganized, expanded legislature, and a huge increase in taxes and tariffs. There was certainly a need for public revenue; the economy could not achieve further growth without a commitment to public infrastructure. The Wodie government adopted a tax system that imitated the US: income taxes that hit the upper class, sales taxes that socked the poor and a long list of protective tariffs. However, Alodia lacked the buoyant economy of the United States, and the new taxes took a heavy toll on growth. To make matters worse, the new public sector failed to invest wisely; public works ended up being accomplished less effectively, in many cases, than previously under the informal, local-volunteerism system.

A major project in Alodia's (and indeed, in Africa's) history was completed in 1968: the building of the Alo Dam across the Jasil River and the flooding of Lake Banneker. This massive hydroelectric project was undertaken with much foreign expertise and borrowed money, and it is debated to this day whether it was more damaging than beneficial. Many thousands of farmers, mainly Mandinka, who lived along the Jasil were relocated. The impact of this huge "social re-engineering" upon other areas was supposed to be favorably balanced by the vibrant new industrial growth made possible by the dam's power. But the economic benefits of the dam — which were considerable — were widely seen as being distributed unfairly, and the large amount of foreign control over the facility (and the subsequent Jasil River Authority) were greatly resented.

Another aspect of the Alodian economy that was complicated by the flooding of Banneker was the mining of aichacite, the brilliant bluish-green gem that was first discovered in 1961, and is found nowhere else in the world. It was found beneath the Atagal highlands to the west of the river, and mined in primitive 100-foot shafts — until the entire area was flooded. Extensive marketing had made the gem popular — and then the flooding of the lake made it all-but impossible to mine. High prices motivated many tragic attempts at mining the gem, in which hundreds of people died. Alodian technology was not equal to the task of securing deep-water mine shafts. Finally in 1981 a French firm was given a long-term franchise to mine the gem. However, aichacite had become one of the rarest and most sought-after gems in the world, and the company's profits far exceeded the price of the leases it paid the Alodian government.

By the mid 1970s, all the promises of Alodian independence, and the new frontier to have been created by the Alo dam, had come to very little, and things were looking very "third-worldish" in Alodia. There had been bad harvests and famines, the gemstone and tourism industries had become stalled, and foreign debt was growing. A guerilla movement took advantage of the US's post-Vietnam isolationist feelings and waltzed rather easily into power in 1975. (It later became evident that although the guerrillas claimed full independence from any other organization, they were supported by both the Alodian Army and the Soviet Union.) The new President, Amil Boutetour, pledged a "brand new day" — a socialist people's republic that would reverse the thievery and divisiveness of the previous decade. At this point Alodia's history began to parallel that of Tanzania. There was massive economic and political restructuring, most of which paid little attention to market discipline. Although there was still widespread graft at the top, the gap between haves and have-nots narrowed. At the same time, though, there was tremendous economic stagnation, and a new round of foreign borrowing. The country's economy was operating at a net loss during this period, continually relying on credit to meet its payments. An informal economy flourished in the countryside, however, and was more or less encouraged by the government, as it had the effect of relieving pressure on the cities.

The Alo Dam

In the 90s, after the Soviet Union fell apart, Alodia's disorganized socialism became almost totally fragmented, and the country adopted an economic policy that was really little more than month-to-month crisis management. The informal economy surged, of course, and drug trafficking became more widespread and important. Control over the aichacite mines was hotly contested and the mines were seized outright by the army in 1999.

During this period, two segments of society functioned quite a bit better than the rest, and gave some reason for hope. One, of course, was the military. As Gen. Akuopha explained in his inaugural speech, the Alodian army started out strong (Jean-

Henri Alo did not stint on national defense) and was enriched by the US, the French, later the Soviets, and still later (it was widely rumored), by the cocaine trade. The army maintained a high level of morale and discipline, and often functioned alongside the national government rather than under it (this was explicitly seen in the army's behind-the-scenes support for the 1975 Boutetour coup). It was fortunate in that although it maintained high levels of preparation for decades, it never had to fight a real war. Military careers were generally considered respectable and desirable. Discipline and secrecy was absolute; the Alodian army was never successfully investigated by anyone either inside or outside the country.

The other area that still functioned tolerably well was the public education system. This probably owed a good deal to the memory of Alo, for whom education was always a top priority, but it also received much attention under the so-called "socialist" Boutetour•regime. Teachers were well-respected and paid surprisingly well, on a par with medical doctors. Alodia achieved the distinction common to some developing countries of being forced to export highly trained personnel because it lacked the jobs to employ them.

Recurring debt crises forced concession to foreign demands for economic restructuring and political openness in the 1990s. A national election was held in 1992, and Jacques Oshodi, a moderate "Social Democrat" was elected. A new constitution was adopted, which established state governments with taxing powers — yet it was clear that political power resided with the Presidency and various Cabinet members with ties to foreign and domestic industry. The familiar imposition of "austerity measures" led to widespread unrest and outbreaks of rioting on many occasions.

The 1990s also saw the emergence of another political force that is, perhaps, unique to Alodia, although its influence appears to be spreading to other countries: the "Christian Coalition." It is unclear what connection this movement has with its namesake in the United States; its activities encompass an eclectic mix of protestant evangelism and native mysticism. Its position on the AIDS crisis — that AIDS is a result of dissolute, un-Christian lifestyles — has created much controversy. It is, nevertheless, an official — and growing — political party, and it has used the media with considerable skill.

The recent coup was the first time in Alodia's history that the Army has taken center stage — although its pervasive influence has always been apparent just beneath the surface. It would seem that some foresighted council of military men sat down during the Alo era and, realizing that instability and insecurity were to be the lot of postcolonial Africa for decades to come, laid their plans for a secure military estate in all weathers. If so, then their success laid the foundation for the latest, most striking turn in the Alodia story.

Down with Akuopha's "Plan"

Editorial — *The Aloville Tribune*, February 1, 2001

One month ago the boys' club that General Samuel Akuopha calls a "government" issued its bizarre blueprint for a new economic order. Alodians should lose no time in understanding the dangers of this most reckless plan and denouncing it for the half-baked fantasy that it is. The plan calls for

— Complete elimination of taxes on income, sales and imports

— Imposition of extremely heavy taxation on only one class: landowners

— Total, immediate repudiation of all foreign debt obligations.

Undoubtedly the removal of taxes and debt obligations will sound good to many people, and bring the coup some interim support. And it does sound good: too good to be true. Alodia has susbstantial debt obligations, but also substantial needs. With all of our social problems, our AIDS crisis, our infrastructure needs, our unemployment levels, we are simply in no position to cut off any chance of international aid. It is the response of a spoiled child — and like a child's tantrum, it will bring punishment.

Nor should we be blind to the outrage of Akuopha's "taxation policy." He asks us to believe that one, and only one, class of citizens is liable for all public funds: those who own land. Has this raving any basis in rational thought? Land owners purchased, or inherited, title to their holdings in good faith. When they use or develop their lands in their own best interests, they allow the economy to progress, and they keep our society from descending into anarchy. Akuopha would have no landowners. He seeks to nationalize all the land of Alodia.

Now, he is sending out teams of "assessors" to assign value to parcels of land across the country. This campaign is being done under strict military control. "No move toward new elections is possible," Akupoha has declared, "until the national cadastre is completed". Teams of so-called "experts" from the Akuopha band will be knocking on your doors, soon, to invade your privacy and "evaluate" your farm. This is the madness that our nation has come to.

Has any government — much less a self-styled regime such as this one — the right to invade the privacy of your own private lands for the purposes of "assessment"? Mr. Akuopha's "assessors" have no legal authority to visit the home of any Alodian citizen. They have no right to expect our cooperation, and they should not get it.

Statement by Rev. Karl Hehner, Christian Coalition Leader

Saturday 24 March 2001. Our community of Faith has prayed and kept silence thus far, seeking guidance on difficult questions, and we have seen where it is written in the Holy Word of God that "The Land shall not be sold for ever, for the land is Mine. Ye are strangers and sojourners with me." We know full well that Satan sometimes comes as a man of peace, but the truth may also be spoken by a man of war, who comes seeking peace: General Akuopha has told us that under his reform program, there will be no market for land, that the land of Alodia will be owned by all Alodians. It is also written in God's word that "Ye shall not work, and another man eat." And we are told that the crime of absentee landlordism shall be abolished in Alodia, and yet honest enterprise shall not be punished by taxation. Therefore we say to General Akuopha that if he tells us the truth, if he and his soldiers are sincere in doing God's work, the Christian Coalition of Alodia shall not resist them: let them look to it!

(leaflet) Autonomous Workers Council

Passed at a public meeting of the committee, 29 March 2001

Workers, what have you to gain from the actions of this general? If he nationalises the land, and taxes at the market rate, then you are paying your rent still, but to the state instead of your landlord. Is this any compensation for military rule? Can you control this nationalised land, vote on how it is used? No. Think on.

What of the squatters, and the landless, now that the state own ALL the land, and has the unalterable final say upon its use, a say in which we as workers have no part! What kind of tool does this put into the hands of the lackies of capital, to move labour around the country as it sees fit, to behave as the lords of the earth, and evict us for any opposition? Workers, do not be dragged into this spat between our masters over who pays for the military machine. Instead, UNITE! Unite to take all the wealth of Alodia into the democratic ownership of all, and resist any attempts for the state to move squatters.

Aichacite: Alodia's Tragic Gem

Aichacite is a gemstone found nowhere else in the world but Alodia's Atagal Highlands. The known lodes are all, now, submerged by Lake Banneker, and mining can only be carried on by expensive, submersible equipment. The story of "Alodia's gem" has more than its share of pathos and mystery — and serves as a sort of catalogue of the problems associated with natural resource management in developing nations.

The gem was rediscovered in modern times in the early 60s under mysterious circumstances. Two men, a Mandinka herdsman named Sunny Matapo, and a Pakistani businessman, Tariq Sahee, recorded side-by-side claims in the Atagal highlands area. The stone was reputedly named for a woman whom Matapo wished to marry. Records of early mining efforts are either anecdotal or nonexistent, but enough of the stones were on the market by 1965 for it to have become highly desired among the "jet set." It was mined, however, in primitive shafts under dangerous conditions. In 1966 the Alodian government issued a series of regulations aimed to restrict aichacite mining to those equipped to safely accomplish it. As a result, supply of the gem increased, and an "aichacite boom" ensued over the next two years.

The stone itself is usually classified as "semi-precious," but that designation is somewhat arbitrary, for its desirability rivals that of such gems as rubies and emeralds, and demand appears to have been kept down by its obscurity and wildly fluctuating supply. It is green in color, with flecks of blue. Its hardness and durability are on a par with the ruby — far more so than the emerald. In any case, it is a beautiful stone. There are hints in legend that the stone's existence was a closely guarded secret long before its modern "discovery," but tribal artifacts in which it may have been used have either been plundered, or kept secret.

When the Alo dam was begun, aichacite miners immediately understood the threat, and mining activity was intense. Fewer aichacites reached the market than might have been expected, however, because of persistent violence over disputed claims. These disputes had been a part of aichacite mining from the start. Astoundingly, the local press suggested that the loss of aichacite mining due to the dam's completion was for the best. For example, the *Aloville Tribune* editorialized, "Whatever else the dam accomplishes, it will afford the benefit of washing out, at least, our murderous avarice over the green stones."

That did not come to pass, however. A half-dozen unsuccessful attempts were made to bring the stones to light during the 1970s. But, Alodia simply did not have the technology to mine gems in submerged 100-foot shafts. Finally the aichacite franchise was awarded to a French firm in 1981, which used ocean research craft to mine the stones. However, the lease agreement that the Alodian government negotiated for the mines turned out to be grossly undervalued. This was, perhaps, understandable, for the gem had brought little but destruction to Alodia for two decades. The new miners, however, deployed a skillfully-wrought campaign to recall aichacite's popularity from the 1960's, fanning the fires of romance and mystery that had always surrounded it. They succeeded, and prices have climbed ever since.

Last October the Alodian Army, in a move now seen to presage their takeover of the Alodian Government, seized the aichacite mines and impounded all the high-tech mining equipment. The government has asserted its right to rescind the ill-conceived lease agreements, and offered compensation to the owners of the equipment. The matter is currently pending under the World Court.

— Morris Chesvian, International Gem Society

Allies Announce Sanctions Against Alodia

Reuters, May 10, 2001 — Paris. Trade ministers of the European Community, the United States, Canada, Japan and Russia today announced their intentions to impose the strictest possible trade sanctions available under WTO rules on the Republic of Alodia. The West African nation, which has been controlled since January of this year by a military junta led by General Samuel Akuopha, has ceased making payments on all foreign debt, and has stated its intention to undergo sweeping land reforms.

In most cases, the sanctions will take the form of a 100% tariff on Alodian products, effectively denying Alodia all of its major export markets. This action will almost certainly reverse the trade surplus that Alodia has maintained in recent years. Should Alodia run even a small trade deficit, the regime would face a liquidity crisis — for, having unilaterally defaulted on all its national debts, it has little chance of securing even short-term financing outside its borders.

The announcement appears to have been timed to create the maximum possible difficulty for the Akuopha regime. The nation's cash reserves are probably close to exhaustion, and General Akuopha's Land Tax program has yet to be implemented. With little possibility of foreign credit, the regime will be hard pressed to meet its current obligations — including the salaries of the Alodian Army, which has been assuming wide-ranging civil-service duties for the last few months. The army's loyalty and discipline is strong by most accounts — but the soldiers have not yet been asked to do without their pay.

General Samuel Akuopha and Dr. Cleopatra Paulin: A Dialogue

Africa Report. **22 April 2001**

On Sunday, we hosted a conversation in our Aloville studio between General Samuel Akuopha, leader of the Alodian Army and head of the Interim Government of Alodia, and Dr. Cleopatra Paulin, the celebrated French physician who has lived and worked in rural Alodia for over two decades. The event, which was Akuopha's first on-camera appearance since his dramatic January 1st announcement, was Africa Report*'s most-watched program ever, widely viewed on three continents. The program had been announced in advance, but with no explanation for the choice of format or participants, except that General Akuopha had sought out Dr. Paulin to be his interviewer.*

Cleopatra Paulin

HOST: So then, first of all a big welcome to *Africa Report.* I'm Bertram Hanno and we are pleased to bring you a very special programme today. We are delighted to have on the stage today, none other than General Akuopha himself. Good day, General.

AKUOPHA: Good day, everyone

PAULIN: Good day, General Akuopha.

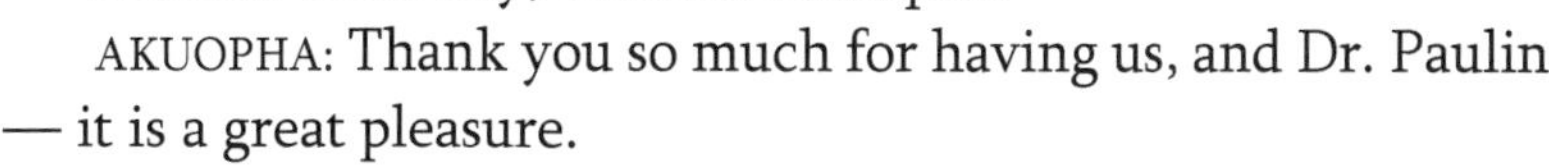

AKUOPHA: Thank you so much for having us, and Dr. Paulin — it is a great pleasure.

HOST: Also joining us is Dr. Cleopatra Paulin, representing the group *Medecins Sans Frontieres.* Greetings, Doctor.

PAULIN: Greetings, Mr. Hanno.

HOST: To start things off, let us ask the General, sir, where have you been hiding for the last several months, and why have you chosen this occasion to face the public?

AKUOPHA: I wouldn't say "hiding" but — last week I issued a rebuke to my staff for the tone of some of their public statements. I have been staying inside, doing my work, letting my temper be contained indoors for the most part. Now that we are on the way to achieving a full roll of land rental assessments for

TO ALL PERSONNEL
FROM SAMUEL AKUOPHA
RE: THE TONE OF OUR STATEMENTS

We received a letter from a certain "village corporation" of Schemefreesi, in Gancha State, thanking Hiram Behele for clarification regarding questions of assessment, and suggesting — rather graciously — that he not adopt a belligerant tone when making such responses. I could not agree more.

When we embarked on our economic reforms, we expected rough treatment from the press, and we have gotten it. We are not statues, and a constant stream of invective has, perhaps, given rise to a seige mentality. Some of us have begun to act as if everyone were against us. And it must stop.

Indeed, I myself have been heard grumbling and cursing at the audacious lies that have been published about us — which is a large part of the reason why I have avoided public statements thus far. If you people make mistakes, I can chastise you, but my gaffes will be prime time news. When I do make my next foray onto the airwaves, in two weeks' time, I will have to be very careful.

We must remember AT ALL TIMES that what we are attempting in Alodia is radically new, that there is little or no public comprehension of our program, and that we can count on the press, in general, to obfuscate more than it makes clear. Therefore we will give the benefit of the doubt to ALL QUESTIONERS. We will respond with patience and forbearance, to the point of meekness, to all questions that are asked.

We must not forget that our regular army personnel are bearing the brunt of all the abuse being hurled by our enemies. Our soldiers can scarcely walk down a public street without someone attempting to taunt or bully them into a violent response. Think of the patience that we are demanding of our front-line men, and HOLD YOUR TONGUES.

Alodia, seems a good time to say a few things about what we are attempting to do. I wanted to keep my feet out of my mouth!

HOST: Dr. Paulin would probably like to address that and some other matters. Doctor, I leave the General to you ...

PAULIN: Thank you, Mr. Hanno. And thank you, General Akuopha for making the time to address some of the issues which concern me. In spite of my outspokenness in recent days, political and economic issues which concern me in Alodia are few and far between —

AKUOPHA: The issues that concern you are precisely those issues that I want to address, first and foremost

PAULIN: except for those which directly affect public health concerns. Thank you, your concern and interest is crucial to resolving these issues. My areas of work in Alodia, as I am certain you know, are childhood immunizations and training for rural technicians and native healers. However, the issues I am most concerned about deal with the plans for extensive rural development projects — and the lack of a public health infrastructure in Alodia. While urban areas are served and some rural areas are served by clinics, the largest number of people in Alodia live in areas with no access to clinics or hospitals. I am concerned that large development projects will exacerbate this problem.

AKUOPHA: I can see how you would be. But there are no plans for extensive rural development projects. Certainly nothing of the inorganic, unnecessary sort of the Alo dam. I wished they had named it something else! Our proposals are not in that vein at all. Rather, we seek to end the unproductive hoarding of good quality, arable land, so that people may put it to appropriate, sustainable use. We need no "green revolutions" or massive imports of farm machinery to accomplish that. We merely need to stop denying people access to farmland. It is my wish and hope that rural development will proceed where needed, no more than needed, and will be *led* by the provision of public health infrastructure.

PAULIN: In rural areas, there is not much arable land that is not currently in use. As you are aware, I spend large amounts of time in remote areas of Alodia. There are problems with some arable land, due to the Alo Dam and the increased standing water brought about by the lake. In particular people will not farm areas near the river where the flow of the water has changed and the black flies breed and cause River Blindness. A lot of arable land has been submerged by the lake, of course, but additional arable land has been lost due to the decreased efforts, due to lack of moneys, at eradication of insect vectors (flies and mosquitoes) nearest the lake. Without a serious battle to clear these lands of insect pests and to provide treatments for the parasites the insects bring, the arable land will be and is worthless.

AKUOPHA: I am well aware of these problems — though I cannot claim to have been bitten by as many flies and mosquitoes as you have! And I know that they will not be solved easily. But let me say that they would never have any chance of being solved, without some sustainable, progressive economic reforms. Economic policy is not your concern, but I am concerned with finding a way to provide for these ecological repairs, among the myriad other ills that need attention in our society. Yes, most of the arable land is being used, but how is it being used? Most large, single crop plantations are not economical, but persist because of subsidy and trade considerations. We could survive without growing the amount of cocoa that we grow. We should remember that Alodia was a net exporter of food in the early 1970s — even after the injuries of the dam.

HOST: Pardon my intrusion, but is there any motivation for the private sector to eradicate insects near the lake? Must it be a purely governmental operation?

AKUOPHA: Today — or, I should say, up until yesterday, in the debt-ridden IMF-hostage scenario, of course there is not. There is very little "private sector" in the Western understanding of that term. Soon, however, I hope there will be a much more vibrant "private sector" with many more options than before. In this case, however, it is obvious to me that the pests are a communal problem, and the public sector will have to work on them.

PAULIN: What could the motivation for the private sector

be? The land is mostly suitable only for small holder subsistence agriculture, river transport for long distances requires commercial boats, not the small pirogues, and the roads are nonexistent to get cash crops to market. The small farmers cannot afford to eradicate the pests, when they cannot afford to keep their children clothed, educated and healthy. Yes, all of Africa was a net exporter of food thirty years ago, whatever the cause of the current situation. But we come again to the Catch-22 — the environmental problems cannot be solved without economic moneys generated by solving the economic problems first. My point is this: economic policies without public health concerns addressed first are killing people. The arable land, not being used near the river, will not be used by subsistence farmers because of the net loss due to disease. Other lands nearer the resettled villages are already being used for cash exports crops.

AKUOPHA: Dr. Paulin —

PAULIN: And, General, with all due respect, you tell me the environmental health problem cannot be solved without first solving the problem of an economy that provides money for it. What I see is, once more, Africans will sacrifice their health for the economic gains of a few.

AKUOPHA: Are we here to list the problems of Africa? How many weeks are allotted for this broadcast? Let me tell you, I would have preferred there be no dam, I would have preferred the Jasil, on whose shores I grew up. The loss of that river was a heartbreak to me as it was to countless thousands of my people. But I begin to see your objections more clearly, at any rate. Always in the past, "economic policies" have meant western-style "capital development projects," imposed on African people and African land without the merest regard for their health and sustainability. Why? because Africa was to be the bargain-basement resource center for the Western economy. Lake Banneker was not designed or made to help the people of the Jasil valley make their own living, to feed themselves, to stay healthy! Lake Banneker was vomited across the Jasil valley so that well-connected landowners could tie into profitable developments. I say to you that you cannot, now, offer any hope of resolving these horrible public-health problems without sustainable economic reform that provides justice to all working people in this country, and that has to begin with our birthright in land. That is what *I* mean by "economic development plan," which seems such an obscene phrase to you.

PAULIN: Sustainable economic reform requires healthy, educated, living people. Blind people will not sustain themselves as easily as the seeing. The diseased will not farm as efficiently as the well. The malnourished will detract from a society, not contribute to it. What sustainable economic reform are you talking about, General? You say no rural development, except to increase use of arable land, but cannot provide protection from the pests on the land. Non rural development will move people about and expose them to more and unfamiliar diseases.

AKUOPHA: Did I say — ?

PAULIN: There is no money for treatment, diagnoses and cures. Is this sustainable?

AKUOPHA: Did I say we could not provide money for protection from the pests? If people are hungry, they must be fed. If they are ill, we must cure them, and the first step toward that is to make sure they have clean water and adequate sanitation. I know what the problems are, Dr. Paulin! But if we want to do more than make speeches to polite applause at the United Nations, then we must consider *how* such things can be provided. How. Should the rich nations simply buy them for us, because we are so helpless? No. We are not helpless in Alodia. Wealth is produced, and stolen, in Alodia. We have a solid public school system, not all is lost there by any means. Our economy has been willfully run in the most *unjust* and *inefficient* way possible, to benefit the few. What we need to do is to allow people to produce what they want to produce. We have been robbed by land-barons, and we have been robbed by banks, and we have put a stop to that. Can I solve all these problems tomorrow? No. Can they *ever* be solved, without a sensible economy? No, no, no! We can kill a lot of bugs with what we have been flushing away in debt service.

PAULIN: I have no illusions about the uselessness of the UN.

In 55 years of moving towards their laudable goals of removing want and hunger and disease, in Alodia and Cote d'Ivoire and Ghana and so many of our other neighbors, they have made all the plagues of man more common, and more dangerous. Let's discuss a specific project. For example, moving small farmers onto arable lands. Riverine lands pose the danger of river blindness and the locals are too scared of losing their sight to farm near the bends in the river. Is there money to pay for black fly eradication? Who will pay for it? Who will provide the drugs? The drug to treat River Blindness is available free to all sufferers from its manufacturer. The problem, as always, is how to pay to get it there, and how actually to get it there, and who will distribute it. Is there money now, when there was not money yesterday? Where is the money to transport the drug?

AKUOPHA: I understand your insistent focus on specific tasks, and I applaud it. Yet you must understand that every such situation bears on the overall economic picture. Now first, please be clear that we have no intention of *moving* anyone anywhere. We aim to provide opportunities, not issue marching orders. But let's assume that people do want to use the land near what was once the Jasil river. The money will be the money that is no longer being paid to Western banks. Or to multinational corporations who own plantations. Or to members of a dozen families who control development and trade in Alodia. Because these are all functions of land rent and monopoly income, which we seek to take for public needs in all cases. And I disagree that the truly deepest problems lie in the logistics of such projects — difficult as they are. The greatest difficulty lies in having the will to do it, and having the resources to accomplish it. You figure out the logistics, that is your expertise. Someone must provide the resources, that is what I am trying to do.

PAULIN: Yes, the logistics is my expertise, because that is often all I do. This is why I keep coming back to the logistics of the situation. I can get the childhood vaccinations from MSF and Bill Gates. They can be delivered to the port. Then I must come up with time, money and means to move them to the rural villages.

AKUOPHA: I believe it is a public responsibility —

PAULIN: While I do a lot of the driving myself, once I get to the more rural areas, this is no easy task with roads that have not been repaired in years. Yes, a public responsibility — but where is the public who has the money and is responsible enough to do it?

AKUOPHA: Not the job of one heroic woman —

PAULIN: You're talking rural people without the means and moneys to get very far to take charge of the situation, General. Again and again, it is the logistics that *must* be overcome before anything can be done. You have an army at your disposal to move the mountain of logistics for you. Most people in Alodia are not so fortunate.

AKUOPHA: The peasants are not responsible for eradicating the black flies! They did not flood the lake! They bear no responsibility for the flies, they just bear the suffering they cause.

[HECKLER]: Repudiate all foreign debt immediately, or else you are a capitalist fascist!

AKUOPHA: Who is this fellow? Have you been living in a cave? We have done that. Kindly sit down. Dr. Paulin, the army can accomplish very little. They can keep the peace while we try to start something positive. They can bear the taunts and assaults without shooting people; they can protect the assessment team from vandals. Can they save all the peasants? Hardly.

PAULIN: Then whose job is it, and what opportunity have you really provided without the logistics to make it happen? I'm not asking the army to save all the peasants. I'm asking for a reasonable opportunity for the peasants to enjoy reasonably good health. There is no opportunity without the health to make it.

AKUOPHA: I realize that, Dr. Paulin. But I bring it up because it is vital that everyone understand this. Alodia's problems — Africa's problems — are too big to be saved by any army, or any philanthropic foundation, or indeed any subset of the people. Our problems can only be solved by removing the barriers that keep our people from cooperating. And I am not — let me be clear — I am not talking about ethnic barriers. I am talking about barriers imposed by an unjust, self-serving political economy.

You see, I want to provide for the logistics of not just eradicating the black flies but also providing clean water. And fixing the roads. And improving the schools. And providing national health care insurance. Yes, that is in our plans! I want to provide for the logistics for free and fair elections. I have no desire to be President of this country! And to provide for the logistics to make sure that well-connected, offshore-funded factions cannot regain their control over government spending. All these matters are important. I cannot afford to save one life while losing whole regions.

PAULIN: I don't want to solve problems, I want to immunize children and train microscopists and provide liaisons with local healers and medical doctors. I don't want to save one life.

AKUOPHA: I want you to teach Alodians to do that!

PAULIN: I want to provide the means for people to live relatively healthy lives.

AKUOPHA: As do I.

PAULIN: Everything I encounter is a roadblock to this. There are microscopes and competent men in the villages who can be trained as technicians and phlebotomists. They can diagnose the diseases.

AKUOPHA: No one understands that better than I, I assure you. I hope to be able to show you a new way of doing business.

PAULIN: Western-trained doctors are learning to work with the native healers, every Alodian's front line of defence against any disease. But you need electricity to use a microscope. You need funds for disposable syringes, only the vaccines are free of cost. You need drugs to treat the diseases diagnosed by the technicians and healers. You need healthy people to run an economy. You need human development coupled with economic development. And you tell me the latter must come before the former. To me this is just another recipe for failure, General. It's hard to be anything but steamed at more words of a bright and shiny future — if only I wait until it occurs.

AKUOPHA: Again with the litany of problems. Dr. Paulin, I was born in the Jasil River valley. I grew up here. I have watched every stage of the pathetic history of the "sovereign nation" of

Alodia. I do not need this catechism. Indeed, every recipe I have ever been offered has failed. I have had friends and relatives die of most of the diseases that you have treated here. It almost seems that people are comforted by portraying Africa as a basket case. That is certainly the conventional "wisdom." But I say to you again, we are not helpless and we do not need to live with our hands out! With all the great respect I have for you and what you have accomplished, I do not want to need your services here!

You are wrong when you say I want economic development to precede human development. That is a failed western model. I want economic development to *be* human development. I want no one in Alodia to be left behind. I want no one to be deprived of opportunities and rights. I believe that when we set free an economy organized along those principles, *we will create, we will distribute* the resources that we need. If I am wrong, heaven help us. But even if I am wrong, at least we did something, before being marched to the firing squad.

PAULIN: General Akuopha, I am well aware that it is preposterous for westerners to think they have the answers to African ills, and to come here with the designs of curing these same ills. In particular, the programs implemented by the NGOs recognize this far better than the UN's method of creating needs that did not exist before. However, the best programs, that allow Alodians to take charge of their own futures, are difficult to implement because of the low level of rural infrastructure. The Alo Dam, as we both know, provides electricity for urban developments, not for rural peoples. There has never been the money for this. Yet, the least electricity in a rural village could mean that most rural peoples could live fairly healthy lifestyles without the need to head for a distant clinic at great expense to money, health and family. With a microscope and a competent native healer, coupled with childhood immunizations the incidence of disease would drop dramatically and life expectancy would rise. I'm not a politician, I have to deal with the concrete; that's all I do. A doctor is trained to find the problem she can cure. I cannot deal in the abstract terms of what will make life better, General, because all I see is how it will be implemented and the roadblocks to the implementation. As a health care professional the roadblocks are always the same. Yes, General, a litany is forthcoming: The need for clean drinking water, electricity, sanitary living conditions, childhood immunizations.

AKUOPHA: These are our first priorities.

PAULIN: Then, when will the wells, where ground water has been contaminated by the lake, be replaced? General Akuopha, it would be of great assistance to my understanding of what is happening if you could tell me something about what development projects you have in mind that the government itself will be proceeding with.

AKUOPHA: I haven't had time to devise specific development projects. As I said before, I am *not* the President of the country, and I have no desire to be. I have taken it upon myself, myself and my advisors, to take hold of a suicidal nation before it does itself in. I am not an expert in any of these areas. While that did not stop previous governments from undertaking disastrous projects, I hope that we can use more wisdom from now on. My job is to set Alodia on a path. If I *were* the President, I would appoint you as the Secretary of Health, and I will certainly recommend that be done. Not to flatter you! But we need the sort of uncompromising expertise and commitment that you have demonstrated. And you know as well as I do that such people are not rare in our country. The logistics are not really our problem.

HOST: And so, we have about one minute before our final commercial break. Any remaining remarks for our viewing audience?

PAULIN: Well, I have lived in Alodia long enough to appreciate that all things eventually change and that some things one must just wait and see.

AKUOPHA: Dr. Paulin?

PAULIN: Bring your children in for their immunizations and see your local healer *sooner* with your health concerns. And thank you for your time, General Akuopha.

AKUOPHA: Thank you! I hope we do not disappoint you.

From a Training Manual Issued to Alodian Troops Tasked to Assist in Land Cadastre

The first necessary step in assessing the value of land is determining who the land belongs to. Yet, our nation typifies much of West Africa in its lack of records. In your home, in the village where your family came from, it is usually clear to those who live there whose farm occcupies what space. Your task is to record this "unrecorded knowledge," You will interview, if possible, every person known to "have land" in the area to which you are assigned. On the aerial-view maps with which you have been provided, you are to record, as clearly as possible, and with as much assistance and input from the local residents as possible, the lines that *the people themselves say* are the boundaries of their lands.

It should be understood from the very beginning that many people will not know what you are doing, and will not trust you. You must never, in any case, offer a threat. At this stage of the project, your task is not to value the land, and it is not to adjudicate ownership of the land. Your task is simply to ascertain, in the words of the people who live there, what pieces of land belong to what people.

You are never under any circumstances to take sides or to become involved in disputes. If rights to some land are disputed among two or more parties, note it. Make a note of what pieces of land are disputed, if you can. Record any information that seems to bear on the question. Then, wish the people a good day and move on.

Famous Orphanage to be Auctioned

***The Aloville Tribune,* July 22, 2001.** The Okeripi orphanage is an oasis amidst the hustle and some times violent bustle of Aloville. But those young, bright and singing faces of late have taken on a solemness reminiscent to them of their own personal hard times.

On nine acres the walled compound has been home and sustenance to the most vulnerable of Alodia's people. Father Mumbura has been a guiding force for not just orphans of disease and misfortune but those 'orphaned' by violence. Over the decades he has used these acres not to just raise food and to teach his "Okeries" the discipline of farm work but also the pride of accomplishment. When the orphanage was first formed it stood nearly alone on the plains and offered a rest stop to those travelling on to what is today the old section of Aloville. Father Mumbura, while not the original founder of Okeripi, has steered its mission through the decades as the city has popped up around him. "There was a time, when at night it would be quiet." he said.

"I have faced many problems living with the city as it formed round about, and for the most part I thought it was God's fortune that we could also have direct access to Alodia's elite in the pursuit of their charity. But now there is nothing that can save us." The elite were there and were stunned by the size of the assessment that has been levied on his operation. "This cadastre is not a boon but a doom. We Alodians no longer can claim our attachment and security to the land when the Government by means of outrageous taxation claims all land as its own." With his voice cracking, "All the reserves that we have built over the years for our dreams and security will in little more than one years time be ravaged by this land tax." Pointing to one of the taller buildings now shadowing his outdoor assembly. "As we here this afternoon find ourselves away from the sun in man made twilight, so to is the bright future of Okeripi covered away by the general's tax regime. We at Okeripi ask so little of the General, we only want to be left alone." After canceling the traditional children's chorus offering of the quarterly event, the emotional gathering then moved to the weathered but original shrine of the Okeripi orphanage and formed a prayer vigil for deliverance. Many of the Okeripi consider the shrine area with its well worn stones a place of strength and emotional refuge.

Some of "big father's" longest supporters were visibly angered to see this community leader humbled so. One little boy pointing to his picture of a monster with a military hat scratched in the dirt, said "General Akuopha is a bad man."

Press Conference, July 23, 2001

Opening Statement of Simon Abiama: The so-called news story published in yesterday's *Aloville Tribune* was inaccurate on many points. We don't wish to ascribe any motives to this, but Dr. Gwarteman and I are here to make sure that the real facts are known.

The article was about the Okeripi orphanage, which for many years has been a beacon of hope in our Capital City. It implied that our government's policies would force the orphanage to leave its home because it was to be levied an inordinately high land value tax. To comfort the little boy who is drawing his pictures of the villainous Akuopha, let us discuss what is actually going on.

We have no intention of forcing the Okeripi Orphanage to leave its home. It is most unfortunate that uninformed reporters — if not outright liars — reached the good Father Mumbura before we had a chance to discuss our program with him. If we had, he would not have been worried.

The assessment numbers used in this article were preliminary cadastre figures for Aloville, which were released yesterday, according to a schedule we announced a month ago. In fact, they were released on time! These are not the taxes that will be charged; they are the assessment team's estimations of the market values of parcels of land in Aloville. It is very hard for me to believe that the *Aloville Tribune* reporters did not know this; if they did not, it could only be because they had failed to read our published statements about how the cadastre would proceed.

Landowners will have a two-week period to review and, if necessary, challenge the assessment figures published yesterday. Now, Dr. Gwarteman will discuss issues specific to the assessment of the orhphanage.

Opening Statement of Dr. Mason Gwarteman: Thank you, Secretary Abiama. I'll be brief, and then take your questions. It is important to remember that Aloville has no formal zoning ordinances or specific land-use rules. These things, of course, are important factors to consider when determining land values. If, for example, these nine acres were enjoined by law or regulation from being developed, that would drastically lower their market value. But, as we understand things, they are not. So we did our jobs, and determined the market value of the site, based on its location and proximity to public infrastructure and services. Because there are no other parcels of land in the city of Aloville that are that size — other than Blakey Park, of course — the assessed value of the Okeripi orphanage was quite high.

In fact, I had a conversation with Father Mumbura which showed me that he understands all this. I visited him, by the way, as a fan of his work, not as an official assessor. He told me that, over the years, he had been approached by developers offering large sums for the orphanage's property. "We have, sadly, sold off bits of our property over the years," he told me, "but we cannot move. This is our home. And we cannot get any smaller, unless we are to deny our children the contact with the land, with growing things, that means so much to them"

I don't know what the government's plans are for cases like this — my job is simply to provide the assessment figures. I can tell you, though, that if the government wishes to leave the Okeripi orphanage exactly as it is, it can simply decide to forego collecting rent on this particular parcel. Considering the level of developments on all sides of Okeripi — and the abundance of vacant or under-used sites that dot the city — I see no good reason to force this excellent organization out of its home.

SIMON ABIAMA: We will take your questions now...

ALOVILLE TRIBUNE: *Is this to be done on a case-by-case basis? Or does the government have a principle for deciding when the tax should be lowered or excused on a particular property?*

MAN IN AUDIENCE: This idea is ludicrous. The ophanage should be moved. The property is worth what the surrounding infrastructure says it is worth. Next thing we'll have a church exemption, and then an old folks exemption. These will be followed quite closely by corporate exemptions because corporations "provide jobs." What total crap. A perfect way to utterly destroy any economic justice.

SIMON ABIAMA: Sir, excuse me, these people have not come here to learn your opinion. To answer the question asked: Exemptions are to be given to bona fide religious and not-for-profit community service entities. Exemptions will ***not*** be granted to for-profit enterprises that are owned by such groups, but only to the service or religious sites themselves. We will ask the new Legislature to strictly define the parameters under which these principles will be applied. There will not be exemptions for individuals or businesses who find themselves paying more tax after the change. I assure you, there will be very few of them.

AFRICA REPORT: *Could you please describe the team of assessors? How many of them are foreign — and how familiar are they with property issues specific to Alodia? Why were foreign assessors chosen?*

SIMON ABIAMA: Thank you for that question. The tale of how our cadastre team was assembled is fascinating, and the process has proved very advantageous for us. We were approached soon after General Akuopha made his New Year's Day announcement by a group of advocates of Henry George's philosophy, offering the services of trained assessors, salary-free. Of course we were happy to accept their offer. Many people do not realize that Alodia has had little or no consistent assessment of real property in its history, at all. There have been property taxes of various sorts in certain cities, but they have seldom been either accurate or consistent. Dr. Gwarteman and his team are training their replacements, who are locally based and are able in their turn to advise them on aspects that are peculiar to land tenure in Alodia.

MASON GWARTEMAN: For my part, and I'm sure I speak for my colleagues when I say that we are thrilled to be part of this momentous undertaking, for I believe that history will not underestimate the importance of our work here. And I would like to add — without, I hope, dragging you into a theoretical seminar — a couple of points. First, we determined that assessments should be based on the land's rental value, irrespective of improvements — and not its selling price. That is certainly the most effective method, if it does not present too many practical difficulties — usually a matter of conflict with long-established practices. But, there were little or no established practices to conflict with in Alodia, so that left us a free field to establish land assessment procedures that will be a good deal more accurate than others that carry, so to speak, a greater weight of political baggage. Secondly, the most significant local characteristic, if you will, has been a general ambiguity about specifically who owns what, in many areas — a rather surprising, to a Westerner at any rate, level of informality in the registration and administration of land titles. The interim government has provided invaluable help with the individual tenure question — which will, of course, bear on market values in many cases. Despite that difficulty, though, after a while it began to dawn on us that we may have stumbled across the very most accurate way to assess land parcels. We ended up breaking valuations up into parcels based almost completely on location, forgetting about property lines — and then cross-checking these findings against the parcel data provided by the cadastral team. We believe that we have created very accurate rental-value maps in this way.

THE POLITICAL ECONOMIST: *There are many people both in Alodia and abroad who doubt your commitment to debt repudiation. It is unprecedented. Is your position unconditional? If not, what sort of refinancing agreements would you consider?*

SIMON ABIAMA: Yes. We are unequivocal on this. The previous administration has considered many refinancing plans and made the requisite guarantees of deep privation of our already struggling citizens. We are done with that, as General Akuopha said: we must now choose another path.

I must add that we have basically recognized a reality that is equally true for any number of so-called developing nations. Alodia was not, in fact, on the lowest tier of hopelessly indebted countries. Indeed, it was in the final stages of securing new relief under the HIPC program, which would have enabled us to eke out a few more painful years in the good graces of Western banks.

The threat of sanctions is real, but the alternative is worse.

Rush Hour in Aloville

A village in the Ashanti Region

Alodian Evening Bombed

***Africa Report.* July 10, 2001.** Offices of *The Alodian Evening*, the nation's second-largest newspaper, were bombed at 2:34 AM last night. Apparently a timed explosive had been placed inside the building. The blast and fire injured at least eighteen people. The employees in the plant were mainly technicians overseeing the nightly press run. The blast seems to have been designed to cripple the newspaper's publishing facilities. Most of the editorial staff was not at work at this late hour, and the blast originated in the printing plant.

The Alodian Evening is alone among the Alodian press in its outspoken support of the Akuopha land initiative. Aloville police detectives examined the wreckage this morning. No suspects have yet been identified.

Coalition of Landowners Refuse Rental Payments

***Aloville Tribune.* June 15, 2001.** Spokesmen for the United Farmers of Alodia (FUA), a coalition of agricultural landholders, announced today that they would refuse to pay the "land rental" bills the Akuopha government planned to send them.

The FUA President, Armand Asmadu, said yesterday that "they collected their information, and we are waiting to see what they will do with it. But this amounts to an illegal confiscation of property. It will force farmers to give up their land — land on which is grown Alodia's major export products. It is illegal, and we will not participate."

The FUA has also called for an immediate restoration of the disbanded national legislature and the ousted President Jacques Boshodi. The Akuopha government has announced plans to hold elections once its economic reforms have been put into effect.

In a statement yesterday, Akuopha spokesman Simon Abiama said that the government would seize the landowners' assets if necessary. "We are not moved by the crocodile tears of this group of very well-placed land barons, however influential they may have been in the past." Abiama went on to reiterate that the value of land, in his view, is the property of all the citizens of Alodia, and that it would be collected by any means necessary.

Mr. Asmadu, however, scoffed at Mr. Abiama's contention. In an interview last evening, he said, "if our members, who, collectively, produce 72% of Alodia's agricultural yield and over half of its exports, are not legitimate farmers, then who is?"

Cadastre Campaign Generates Resistance, Confusion

Aloville, July 8th (Reuters) — In one of the oddest chapters yet in the often circus-like interplay of West African politics, a civil-disobedience campaign is being waged in the capital city against a government team of real-estate assessors. Landowners are claiming unconstitutional violations of privacy. A group of business-suited protesters sought to bar the assessment team entrance to the Aloville city limits on February 20th. The assessors were, however, under full military guard. Resistance was more symbolic than it was effective; no shots were fired, and no one was injured. Twelve protesters were taken into custody and released later that day.

Although the civil-disobedience campaign has gotten considerable play in the press — the nation's largest paper, the *Aloville Tribune*, even went so far as to advocate it in an editorial — its effect so far has been minimal. Nevertheless, a coalition of business leaders and employees of the ousted Oshodi government staunchly opposes the junta's tax-reform and land assessment initiative. "Not only is our privacy being invaded," charged Aloville businessman Paul Otonso, "but our so-called 'rent' charges will be based on the arbitrary decisions of this irresponsible team of who knows who, traveling around with Akuopha's gangs applying numbers to our properties. They are not accountable. No one understands what they are doing, and nobody decided to do this, except for the madman Akuopha."

Whatever one makes of the charge that the valuations are inaccurate or biased, the charge of privacy violation has not stuck. The assessment team's destination that Friday, when they scuffled with Aloville's executives, was the office of municipal records. In fact, the assessors maintain that they have no interest in entering any private building in Aloville. "We are assessing the unimproved value of land." stated Dr. Mason Gwartemann, the US volunteer who leads the team. "In a city, that site value is a function of location, of proximity to traffic and services. We don't need to enter homes to quantify those variables; all we have to do is look at a map, and tour the city streets." Gwarteman also dismissed charges of bias. "We have every hope that General Akuopha's initiative will succeed — which it could not, if we were to cook the books. We don't even know the players. That is the advantage in using an international, volunteer-based team. If we have any allegiance at all in this, it is to the sound principles of public finance that are getting a long-overdue test in Alodia."

Such rhetoric fails to persuade Gerald LaLiberte, the French developer who holds a number of properties in Aloville and the Atlantic resort city of Kahpri-Moloj. LaLiberte announced plans, prior to the recent coup, to contribute to the funding of an Aloville Convention Center, and to build a new resort hotel and casino in Kahpri-Moloj. He claims that the Akuopha government cannot succeed in their attempt to tax something that does not exist. "They claim they want to collect the full rental value of the land," he argues, "But from where will that value come? What will create it? The projects that I, and other developers, will build. Where else could it come from? But by so drastically increasing the carrying costs on these properties, they ensure that we cannot build." LaLiberte joins a growing chorus of high-level commentators who are perplexed by Akuopha's program.

Some commentators do seem to get what Akuopha is up to. "Clearly, Akuopha has gotten his hands on a copy of Henry George's *Progress and Poverty,*" wrote *Slate* Editor Michael Kinsley last week. "But what is remarkable about his plan is that he seems to be attempting to institute George's reform lock, stock and barrel, just the way George wrote it in the 1880s. A noble attempt at sweeping reform, but in the 21st century, how can he succeed?" Similarly, a number of economists — most notably British Nobelist Alfred Warsham — have declared that Alodia cannot meet its budgetary needs with a mere levy on land values alone. According to IMF spokesman Harvey Rugla, the Akuopha plan is "a policy of economic suicide."

Nor is it easy to get a clear reading on the feelings of ordinary Alodians about the new policy. Responses in the press have been overwhelmingly negative toward Akuopha and his plan; indeed, a number of new tabloids have emerged, exuberantly heaping the most scathing criticism on every aspect of the new government, its plans, and even members' personal habits. The *Aloville Tribune* has made no secret of its scorn for the land-tax and debt-repudiation plan. And billboards have started appearing along Highway 9, the thoroughfare that runs from Aloville to Gancha in the northeast, with messages like, "Beware all who have nothing but your land! That is all that Akuopha will tax!"

However, there is a growing feeling that as long as the army stays on its good behavior — which by all accounts it has so far — and the press is left alone to lambaste Akuopha all it wants, many people will be disposed to give the new regime a chance. "The other leaders, every one of them, could never stand criticism," commented Akari Dobon, an Aloville merchant. "Anyone who spoke up might get tossed in jail. But Akuopha, he says, say whatever you like! I'm not too hopeful, but — if he is so unafraid of the press, who knows? Maybe he is honest. That would be refreshing."

— The Republic of Alodia —

October 21, 2001

Gerald LaLiberte, President
Ivory Developers, Ltd.
Dear Mr. LaLiberte:

Your inquiry regarding development in Kahpri-Moloj is most welcome, and has received the most careful consideration.

Of course we welcome the building of new resort properties in this city. The two sites you mention are ideal for this sort of tourism-oriented development, and they have stood idle for a long time. Therefore, for many reasons, we have nothing but support for any new buildings, provided only that they fit the existing building codes of the city of Kahpri-Moloj regarding egress, fire prevention, and public safety in general.

You suggest, however, that these developments cannot be profitably done without the security provided by long-term leases. But this is a kind of security which, alas, we are not prepared to offer. Nor do we believe that development cannot profitably be accomplished without it. So that we may understand each other clearly, please indulge to consider my reasoning on this matter.

The rental value of sites in Kahpri-Moloj would reasonably be expected to increase should other developments of this kind take place — a likely eventuality. By securing a long-term lease at a fixed rate, the developer may, in effect, be protected from increased rental values over the period of the lease.

We are endeavoring to create a rent-as-revenue system for Alodia. We do not, therefore, believe that such long-term leases are in our local or national interest.

The impossbility of fixed-rate leases will tend to dampen rental values for sites. Therefore, the difficulty that you seek to surmount by obtaining a long term lease is, effectively, removed. You can control a site for a lower annual payment than before, and speculative volatility will be dampened. We believe that this will make smaller, more affordable developments feasible, and that this can only serve to enhance the long-term prospects of Kahpri-Moloj as an attractive and affordable place to visit.

Therefore the requirement for land tenure in Kahpri-Moloj, as in all of Alodia, will be the payment of the annual rental value of the site, exclusive of all improvements. To reiterate: we believe that when this system is in effect, the wild price swings of real estate bubbles will cease, and rental values will increase only as locational benefits increase. The imposition of the annual site rental will not be a hardship to any normally profitable business. And more important, the opportunity to run businesses in this tax-free climate will remove much of the burden that currently makes businesses so risky. We believe that investors in development in Alodia under our new site-rental system will be well-rewarded, and we urge you to consider the potential of this new idea.

Sincerely,
Hiram Behele
Undersecretary for Economic Development

Televised on *Africa Report*, June 22, 2001

Q: General Akuopha, what is your reaction to US Secretary of State Colin Powell's staying away from Alodia during his Africa trip?

A: My reaction? I have none. The United States has made its policy toward Alodia clear. We expected no visit from Colin Powell. We heard a great deal of rhetoric about "democracy" and "transparency", while the Secretary visited his most obsequious African friends. No, we were not surprised that his political agenda left no time for him to visit Alodia, but later administrations may react differently.

Akuopha off to China

***Africa Report*, August 5, 2001.** The Head of State of The Republic of Alodia, Gen. Samuel Akuopha leaves for China this evening on the invitation of his Chinese counterpart President Deng Xia Ping.

During the visit he is expected to sign several accords of bilateral relations with Peking and also to receive the full support of Peking to his regime. It is noteworthy that this is the first foreign visit the General is making since he took over power eight months ago.

The General, who is expected back in Aloville next Sunday, shall make a brief stop over in Bonn on his way back to confer with Chancellor Schroeder.

Economic Reform: Not a Job for Amateurs

Op-Ed by Hudson Bonner, *New York Times*, 7 September 2001

The most common theme in the international response to General Akuopha's coup in Alodia has been bemusement, but much of that was disingenuous. Akuopha's reform platform has two major planks: an immediate default on international debts, and a public revenue shift from a conventional tax policy (or, more precisely, a "third-world" version of tax policy, emphasizing import duties, VAT and punitive levies on various disfavored industries) to exclusive reliance on a land-value tax, the old "single tax" idea of Henry George. Most commentary has focused on the wild impracticability, even perversity, of this plan. And, in fact, Akuopha's plan is wildly impractical — but not for the reasons that are usually given.

Debt repudiation would be the obvious choice for a developing nation, if only it could position itself to endure the repercussions. While a few nations, notably Peru and Colombia, have attempted to dictate terms to their creditors, Alodia is the first attempt a complete, unilateral default, a step Harvey Rugla called "a policy of economic suicide." But is it? Alodia has (of necessity) run a trade surplus for some years. If the public revenue program gets off the ground soon enough, then Alodia would have an outside chance of weathering its liquidity crisis. If it managed that, then it could be free, in effect, to thumb its nose at Bretton Woods. That, of course, is the bankers' worst nightmare. It would start other developing dominoes thinking of more productive ways to spend the money they currently dump into debt service. If we keep these facts in mind, the rather extraordinarily vindictive level of economic sanctions adopted this week — against, after all, a tiny player in world trade terms — makes sense.

Akuopha's second plank, however, is more problematic. It seems as though the General and his team have read no more economics than Henry George's *Progress and Poverty* (1879), and decided simply to put George's plan into effect, to "abolish all taxes save that on land value," Laudable, but foolhardy:

if Alodia wants to build a functioning modern economy, it can ill afford to ignore the economic insights of the last 122 years. Alodia is (to use the current euphemism) a "Less Developed Country." As such, it must have capital formation — and therefore it must have a healthy financial system (something that, admittedly, few LDCs can boast). In short, if Alodia is to grow, then its entrepreneurs must have access to funds. One insight that Henry George failed to grasp is that growth does not happen instantaneously. It will not help for economic activity to be freed from tax burdens if that activity has not yet taken place, and will not take place without some form of financial pump-priming. Alodia has placed itself in a vicious circle.

Real estate provides the overwhelming majority of the collateral assets upon which loans are based. If Alodia's economy is poised for healthy rates of growth, the projected capital gains from real estate make such loans good bets, which serves to fuel entrepreneurial expansion. Yet this is exactly what the Akuopha regime, by taxing away all of land's rental value, would take out of private hands. Where will Alodia's venture capital come from? Not from international investors, certainly. Where else, then, can it come from but the government itself? Is General Akuopha even aware that he is leading his nation into a planned economy?

The repudiation of unsustainable — and unjust — international debt burdens is a rational step, which is a fact that International Finance will have to face up to, sooner or later. And, the shifting of tax burdens off of productive enterprise and onto the surplus revenue of landowners is also a sensible step — if it is adopted rationally and gradually so as not to fatally shock the economy it is trying to save. However, for a military junta to attempt to implement untried, theoretically questionable economic policies is the height of irresponsibility. Akuopha appears not to understand the risk he is taking. If his policy fails, the resulting chaos may not be controllable by any army.

(Hudson Bonner is Klingelhoefer Professor of Political Economy at the New School of Social Research. His most recent book is Required Jubilee: The Debt Crisis and Global Sustainability)

Letter to the Editor, *New York Times*

Show me the money!" I am told this was a line from a movie starring Tom Cruise, but I have not seen the film. Prof. Bonner is correct: banks will not do business in Alodia as they did before. Their ability to bleed people dry will be severely restricted. We will probably need to move to a new kind of bank. The short-term answer — which Dr. Bonner, rather disingenuously, I suspect, did not mention — is microcredit. Small loans to poor people, especially women. The Grameen Bank has shown us that this model works. In Alodia, with the blooming of small business that is about to happen, it has never been a better investment. — Mason Gwarteman, Ph.D

Migrant Worker Pattern Changes

The Alodian Evening, December 5, 2001. The standard annual influx of seasonal workers from Mali and Burkina Faso to Alodia's cocoa plantations and other farms is underway — but it is proceeding quite differently than usual. In past years, an estimated 30,000 workers have come into Alodia for seasonal employment, and then gone back home.

This year, the demand for seasonal workers is much lower than in the past, because of the decline in large-scale cocoa plantings and general agricultural shift caused by impending land and tax reforms. However, many men, disappointed by having made their long summer's trek seemingly for nothing, have been moving on to find other work in Alodia.

Instead of their accustomed jobs on the cocoa plantations, workers have been finding employment on newly-established small farms. It seems that many new farmers had made ambitious plantings and now need extra help to get their crops in. Other migrant workers have heard through the grapevine of opportunities in the hotels and casinos of Kahpri-Moloj, which is enjoying its most prosperous tourist season in history.

Many Alodians worry that if the current economic upturn continues, a surge of immigrants willing to work for low wages could wipe out opportunities for Alodians themselves. A number of editorialists have called for immigration restrictions. No word on this question has yet come out of the Presidential House in Aloville.

Reclaiming our Future: A Response to the Public Questions of Monique Sassafras

Recently a woman named Monique Sassafras began a series of public critiques of Alodia's interim government and its economic reforms. Regrettably, she was rudely and inappropriately ridiculed in public by an employee of the interim government. At about the same time, Monique Sassafras distributed a handbill that forcefully states her grievances against our program. We believe that her questions are important and deserve the most serious consideration. We also believe that we can satisfy her misgivings on each point that she raises. But you, the citizens, shall judge. Her statement is reprinted verbatim here, with our comments interspersed. — The Interim Government of Alodia, General Samuel Akuopha

Monique Sassafras

I think that western ideas ought to be experimented on western peoples. That Georgism has never been applied to the macro-economy of a western nation makes me wonder why it should be applied to the macro-economy of Alodia. Is Africa some laboratory for western philosophies?

It is not surprising that Georgism has never been applied in full in any Western nation. It is a radical philosophy; it seeks to remove the root cause of poverty. And, although Henry George was an American and came out of the European intellectual tradition, it is not altogether accurate to characterize the Georgist philosophy as "Western." Georgist economics is grounded in basic economic behavior that is observed in every society. In fact "Western" societies have turned away from the fundamental insights Georgism offers about just and sustainable economic development. And we are seeing no friendliness from today's "Western" countries toward our forthright adoption of Georgist principles.

Does our fearless leader consider, in his passion for this experiment, the culture, the history, the identity of the people of Alodia? No, instead he insists that the system will be for a nation without tribal boundaries. Alodia is NOT a nation without tribal boundaries. Like the rest of equatorial Africa, Alodia is an artificial nation carved out of the jungle to serve the needs of whatever Europeans could survive long enough off the coast to take what they wanted and return nothing but contempt for the people they stole from. People in the north are very different from the coastal peoples. Different groups have their own history, their own languages, even for the many who also speak French, their own customs handed down and preserved by the women of the family for generations. Does Georgism account for this? The results of this experiment will not be available overnight, unless the experiment fails. They will be something that is felt in the future, if it is successful. In the meantime, what is happening that is different today? Or for my children? (If I say "my", I am accused of being greedy and making it all for me. If I say "our", I am accused of speaking for others without their permission.)

This is the most serious question that we have had to face. It cannot be denied that Alodia's boundaries were created by Europeans for European reasons. This has caused decades of suffering. We cannot impose — or have imposed on us — a western model of democracy that fails to account for cultural, religious and philosophical differences among groups of people, forced to live within arbitrary lines slashed across their ancestral homes. This is one of two things that we can never forget.

What is the second? That despite its disadvantages, its colonial legacy, its arbitraryness, the nation-state is the entity that we have to work with. Sovereignty, in today's political reality, resides with the nation-state. We cannot go back to edens past. We cannot create "autonomous tribal homelands." We MUST NOT resort to "ethnic cleansing."

You ask whether "Georgism" accounts for this. In order to answer that question meaningfully, we would have to be clear on what we understand the tenets of Georgism to be. For now, we can say this: social harmony is possible in a pluralistic society that respects basic justice; social harmony is impossible in a homogenous society in which human rights are not respected.

Finally, you ask what is happening that is different already, today. It takes time to shift the course of a nation's economy. But indeed you can already observe some changes. The previous government jailed dissidents and shut down opposing voices. We have defended and encouraged free speech and free assembly. Even the so-called "harrassment" of Monique Sassafras was no more than impolite shouting. She was not touched, jailed or abused. Merchants and buyers have also noticed, incidentally, the removal of the stinging flies of taxation on many of the things they buy and sell.

Most western economic principles flow from Adam Smith and his invisible hand free market ruling the world. In Alodia, people with families, as most people in Alodia are, cannot afford to act entirely in their own self-interest at all times, because the self-interest of the individual has a history which includes the self-interest of the family. For example, a good marriage serves the tribe and the family. In western societies marriage is often for the interest of the individual couple only, with near kinfolk excluded from even attending the wedding ceremony. Marriage in my family is a tribal affair. Everyone comes, including your houseguests, all of your extended family, their children and etc. Ultimately one can say that anything anyone does is in their self-interest — for example, in Africa appeasing one's family duties is in one's best interests. Then Adam Smith's phrase becomes meaningless and is reduced to pointing out that what happens is what happens.

> *We will leave philosophical debate to another forum. There is much to consider, however, in the question of whether it is appropriate to employ "Western" economic policies in Africa. One fact that must be addressed, for example, is the prevalence of traditional, non-monetized ways of doing business. There are many, many people in Alodia who have no "assets" at all in any Western sense of the term, yet who make their living, raise their families, contribute to their communities and their culture. To force an industrial, hourly-wage model on such people is to dehumanize them. That is not the path to development that we will take. Monique Sassafras wonders whether there is any other path. We believe there is.*

What is it about Georgism that will bring equality of justice to Alodia? As I have pointed out many times, the land is and has been, for many years, in the hands of people who have been sucking a profit off the backs of villagers who once owned the land. The crops grown by those villagers who have kept their lands have been paid for at below market value for many years. Now it is pointed out that equality of access to land is being striven for.

Those people who lost their village lands to forced development to make room for shanty towns for the mines or crop land for the miners, or resorts or whose lands are drowned by the dam are in a financial situation that guarantees they can continue only to work for others and will never have money to access land. Why would anyone with land give it up? Those people who have been underpaid due to bribes given to non-elected officials receiving structural adjustment moneys from *Bank Mondiale* are also not in a position where georgist land policies will be of benefit to them. There will be no greater access to land before than after.

This — fortunately — is not the case, a fact which the "United Farmers of Alodia" know only too well. There is egregious waste of good land in Alodia. Vast acreage is now devoted to crops grown for export, grown in the most harmful and polluting manner, and whose profitability demands a ready supply of cheap labor. This was seen as a necessity by a series of regimes desperate to earn foreign exchange to meet debt obligations. We are no longer bound by such arrangements. Heretofore, these large planters — as well as resort developers — have not been required to contribute to public welfare in any way whatever; on the contrary, they received subsidies. Their water and fertilizer was often free; their equipment was often bought with money borrowed from the West. Planters know quite well that once they are required to pay their fair share — the value of the land that they have monopolized — and denied these egregious handouts, they will make no money growing cocoa. They will take their stolen money and run, leaving Alodia with a generous supply of arable land, there for the taking.

My children will continue to be deprived of access to land (and how dare the government send its spokesman to call me lazy and worthless, I make a living for my children and myself) as long as the word is that past injustices will not be addressed. This is one reason for not supporting the current government. When Jobe yells at me that I am in the wrong for not blindly buying any offer of a different future he is confused. First, show me a reason to believe. Alodia has gone from bad to worse in the post colonial days in spite of a number of advantages on the West Coast of Africa in general, mosquitos, education, lower AIDS rates.

Now, Alodia is securing the position of the land thefts. How does this equate to land justice? Alodia is giving its official seal to these thefts by saying all the current "owners" have to do is pay for the use and the land will be theirs. Isn't this what is going on? In order to build infrastructure in Alodia, native growing lands were converted to single crop export agriculture to earn cash to pay for loans, roads, hospitals, and schools. There is finite growing land available in Alodia and even less than before with the flooding of prime river lands. Women of my family who own cocoa fields profit from them, but have not been paid market value for the beans for years. They have, however, paid market price for everything they need to grow and maintain the cocoa. Their profit is not available to pay the market value assessed tax on their land. The government has sown their profit into the earth to build airports. If they cannot pay the taxes, then who will own their fields? Whoever can pay the taxes? Well, who can pay the taxes? The cash crop exporters who have profit in abundance from dealing with the illegal (was and is) government of Alodia in the past.

The real coup is the legalization by the present government of the theft. It negates the future need to steal.

> *Those cash crop exporters will either be gone, or paying their share for the community, as never before. Lands that were converted can be reconverted. We believe that it is a lie to say that people must trade their land and their culture for development and infrastructure. We believe that that was never necessary. Much harm has been done by the exploitative economic system that has had, at its very root, the Western concept of private ownership of land! So who are the thieves of our land? Did not the current owners simply buy or inherit their land from earlier thieves? We believe that ANY private ownership of land in the "fee simple" model — without, in other words, a social responsibility to satisfy every person's equal right to land — is thievery. This is something that our ancestors knew. In their attempt to enslave us and steal our birthright, Europeans taught Africans a "modern" theory of development in which everything in the world, even land, even human beings, is bought and sold. But their doctrine of the commodification of the natural world is an abomination.*
>
> *What has all this to do with economic reform in Alodia? We need not pay tribute to an economic system that dehumanizes us and steals our future. But, as you say, we must be*

judged on results. So I ask you to wait one summer, and observe the changes.

We have made many general statements in this brief message, and if Ms. Sassafras and her friends are true to past form, they will demand specifics. And indeed, specifics are available. The land assessment rolls for every city and farm in Alodia are on public view, and the methodology used in the assessment process is available in public libraries and on the Internet. Resources on Georgist economics are widely available and we will supply a bibliography to anyone who asks for one. The press at all levels has carried on lively debate and analysis of every minute stage of our program since its inception and not one page or broadcast — no matter how scurrilous or insulting — has been suppressed. We respect the concerns of Monique Sassafras and all other Alodians and we will continue to do our best to address them, without reservation.

Conference re: Monique Sassafras

In the presidential office, August 10, 2001

AKUOPHA: It has to be a real position, not ceremonial.

ABIAMA: But what qualifications does she have?

AKUOPHA: At least as many as you or I, my friend — you at least are good looking. Hiram, what was the title you suggested?

BEHELE: Undersecretary for Nonformalized Economic Issues. Stop rolling your eyes, Simon — I know it doesn't have a good beat, and you can't dance to it, but it is accurate. And a tall order.

AKUOPHA: She will have advice as good as we have.

BEHELE: She will have a position at the same level as Simon and I — coming in at this late date. And — I might add — much higher than Jobe.

AKUOPHA: My friends, as much as it pains me to admit it, there is a great deal that you have not gotten yet.

ABIAMA: Mainly her job will be to communicate, then.

SPOOK: Who knows, she draws impressive crowds in the market. She may challenge you for the Presidency!

AKUOPHA: If she does her job well, she should have the Presidency.

ABIAMA: I don't follow.

SPOOK: Of course you don't. That's why you are so useful, politically.

BEHELE: He's right. We are giving her the hardest job of all.

The Sorrows of Jobe

Jobe Akalota was a legal scholar and college professor in the Central African Republic. He was imprisoned and brutally tortured in the 1970s after publishing a series of articles critical of that country's dictatorial leader, Jean-Bedel Bokassa. When Bokassa was overthrown by a French-backed coup in 1979, Akalota was released, and he came to Alodia, where he secured another teaching position. He was an enthusiastic supporter of Alodia's "Land Government" and was offered a position on Akuopha's team as a constitutional advisor.

In the early rainy season of 2001, Jobe visited the Aloville market seeking an encounter with Monique Sassafras, who had been speaking out to considerable numbers of people against the Akuopha regime and its activities. He got into a number of shouting matches with Sassafras in the market, which were extensively covered in the anti-Akuopha press. Akuopha called Jobe on the carpet — while he simultaneously offered Monique Sassafras a job in the Interim Government. Jobe's resignation letter, and Akuopha's response, follow.

Dear Akuopha,

Recent events have revealed to me a profound difference in our visions for a peaceful Alodia. I at first thought we were lucky to have the peaceful kind of political transition that enables the most patient and wisest to rise to the top and direct the country with level heads untrammeled by the passions of more violent political upheaval. I have no doubt that you dear Akuopha still meet those critical standards. It is myself that I have doubts for.

My own life has been visited by passions, and I have grown an aversion to them, perhaps irrationally so. When taunted and disrespected like I have been recently, my nights are filled with the visions of my powerless past and the inward rage reawakens. Correcting my failing is an inner struggle which I alone can fight. But the struggle makes me unfit for the delicate and demanding work that Alodia needs. My continued presence would only be contentious with myself and disruptive of the process. Therefore I immediately resign my position as constitutional adviser.

Yours in Peace
Jobe Akalota

Dear Jobe,

I receive your resignation with sadness, and yet with some good hope. You appear not to believe that the regime which I am now leading will be exactly what I have always insisted that it be called: an interim government. We won't be in business much longer; there is little for you to resign from. Now, I do not doubt that you are skeptical of this, and indeed there is no precedent for promises such as this ever coming true. So you will have to let history be the judge. I do say to you, though, that a man possessing such a degree of knowledge and of passion as you will be of great value to Alodia, and will no doubt find a useful and creditable role to play in the permanent government that is to come — which will, I fervently hope, be freely elected by Alodia's people.

Thank you for your distinguished service, and best of luck to you.

Yours in Hope,
Samuel Akuopha

In the presidential office, August, 2001

SPOOK: (handing Jobe's letter back to Akuopha) He is a curious character. More of an evangelist even than Sam here — and *much* more pure.

ABIAMA: What was he doing in the market? What was he trying to accomplish?

BEHELE: He heard that this Monique Sassafras woman was articulate and had a following, and she was denouncing the land government —

AKUOPHA: Which was no big surprise, because it sounded outlandish to her.

SPOOK: Oddly, I suspect the pun was unintentional.

BEHELE: And he felt the need to educate her.

AKUOPHA: He must have seemed completely incoherent. To the people in the market, I mean. It must have sounded like Chinese to them.

SPOOK: Alas, impeccable as the good Jobe is in matters of theory, he has not the charisma nor the stage-presence of Sassafras, and he was reduced to a hissy fit. The *Blade*'s photo of him was priceless.

ABIAMA: This amuses you?

SPOOK: (laughter) Oh, it does indeed! (calming down) And I think it also amuses the General, though his cards are held as close as ever.

AKOUPHA: Jobe is a hothead and romantic. Don't you have work to do?

SPOOK: I am doing it. Like all the best political advisors, I am dutifully playing court as the Fool.

General Samuel Akuopha reluctantly took questions at a demonstration in the "private town" of Schemefreesi.

Jean-Henri Alo's motto for the newly-independent nation of Limbotho was revived by Akuopha's "interim government."

Alodia's Adventure: One Year In

The Political Economist. **January 2002**

It has been a year since General Samuel Akuopha shocked the world with his announcement of a daring new path for the nation of Alodia. It was not at all surpising, of course, that a military junta had taken control of the government, for such things are all-too familiar in African politics. The shocker was the shape of the program that Akuopha announced: immediate stoppage of all foreign debt payments (not a hiatus, but an outright refusal), immediate stoppage of all tariffs and VATs, and the formation of a national land-value cadastre in preparation for a resource-rent system of public revenue.

A new road?

After the September terrorist attack on the US, the Alodia story was among those that the world seemed to forget. This was not necessarily bad for the regime and its agenda. Indeed, the spontaneous outpouring of sympathy and support from Alodians to the people of the US, particularly from the large evangelical community, was really impossible for the US administration to disparage. President Bush himself had to shake the hands of Aloville fire-fighters at Ground Zero. Behind the scenes, US opposition to the Alodian regime remained strong. European allies maintained their alliance with the United States in refusing any commerce with Alodia (despite considerable opposition in France, which was itself blunted by the focus on the war against terrorism).

The regime faced two principal early dangers, one financial

and the other political. Both have abated significantly in recent months. The financial danger was the prospect of a liquidity crisis brought on by a lack of incoming public revenue combined with a reduction of exports. This seems to have been averted, but by a narrow margin. Announcement of a trade pact with China was a key element here — but it is not completely clear how the regime managed to pull together enough money to meet the army's payroll. In previous years it was thought that borrowed money had been used for that purpose, along with such tax revenues as were available — but, both of those sources dried up immediately after January, 2001. Most estimates held that money already in the treasury would maintain operations for the first three or four months, and it is known that land-rent payments would not coming in for at least a few months, and probably a full year. Evidently the "interim government" managed to make up the difference, but exactly how they did it remains a mystery. Indeed, this mystery may be discomfiting to the Akuopha regime; its critics have repeatedly alleged that some form of drug-running, possibly in the form of cocaine shipments to the US, provided the extra funds. Although these allegations have not been substantiated, it is not likely that they will go away while the regime's books appear not to add up.

The early political danger had to do with organized opposition among landowners and corporations. This movement got considerable play in the Western press, but it actually had little popular support. Demonstrations that appeared strong to Western TV viewers were widely understood by Alodians to be staged, with "demonstrators" hired from among West Africa's huge population of migrant laborers. There were bombings: the office of Akuopha's land assessment team in Gancha, and the plant of *The Alodian Evening*, the only paper in the country that expressed support for Akuopha. It became evident that the "movement" in protest of the land reform was more PR than popular.

One factor that greatly benefitted the regime was its steadfast adherence to its free speech policy. Akuopha announced again and again, from the very beginning of his tenure, that no speech of any kind would be suppressed. A number of publications appeared, bitterly critical of Akuopha and his advisors, who were taunted with all manner of sensationalist stories. Not only were there no reprisals, but in some cases soldiers were tasked to make sure that delivieries of certain papers were free from hindrance. These soldiers, in turn, were taunted and, in one memorably televised instance, doused with catsup — but their assailants were not even arrested. This, of course, played well in the eyes of foreign observers, and had a good deal of influence on the pro-Akuopha groups in France and in other Francophone African countries.

In many ways, the centerpiece of the regime's first year was its rather audacious determination to assess the market value of all the land in the nation. Nothing like it had been attempted before — yet the national land assessment program was, on balance, far more successful than anyone predicted. There were many appeals, and many disgruntled voices. In general, however, the only heavy losses the program imposed were on the large industrial farms, most of which were foreign-owned anyway, and they had little popular sympathy.

Aloville firefighter Laurent Akibe appears in the background of this video still of George W. Bush's "Bullhorn Speech" on September 14, 2001

The Alodian assessment team faced the difficult task of supplying land valuations in many places where records were conflicting or nonexistent. The Army actually dispatched soldiers into the field to collect data. Soldiers were sent to places where they knew the people, and they were told to figure out who owned what pieces of land. They were given maps and tasked with piecing together a jigsaw puzzle of land parcels. Then, a team of assessors determined the rental values of those parcels, and the land cadastre was published.

After the appeals process was completed (which continued through December, and many cases still await resolution), any improvements on the land parcels, as delineated in the national cadastre, became the absolute legal property of the landholders, who were issued legal documents to that effect. Furthermore, this deed entitled them to secure tenure on the land that they occupied, provided that they paid their land rent (if any) to the local government.

It is not difficult to see how this program would infuriate large landowners, especially absentees. The chain of events leading up to the breaking of Alodian latifundia, although bizarre and counterintuitive, made economic sense. Where farmland had been used for export-crop production, it was assessed accordingly and rent was charged to owners. Suddenly the owners were in a double bind. Their lands were smacked with a large holding cost, just as international trade sanctions removed the marketability of their crops. In effect, their lands were expropriated — not by soldiers, but by the market. Suddenly large tracts of arable land were available. The land then reverted (in a rather sloppy, evolving manner) to the workers. But, those small farmers, growing either subsistence crops or products to be traded in local markets, could not hope to meet rent payments based on cash-crop exports. They appealed the assessments, and the assessors determined the land now had little or no cash value in its present use. Also, in areas where traditional models of land tenure still held some influence, this process may have contributed to a renewal of interest in tribal and village traditions regarding land tenure.

Some large farms, however — especially those owned by Alodians — continued to find it profitable to grow export crops. Therefore, Alodia managed to earn some foreign exchange (its manufacturing sector, although it did expand, still adds negligibly to exports). So although exports were down, the benefit of exports to the nation's economy seems to have increased — mostly because foreign exchange was no longer siphoned off for debt service.

On paper, it did not appear as though the Alodian experiment had had much effect. Using conventional measurements such as per capita GDP, balance-of-trade or public revenue flows, economic activity in the country seemed to have dropped. However, one certainly did not see anything that looked like a recession in the streets of Aloville, the countryside, or the beachfront in Kahpri-Moloj. Although few statistics were kept, there was a marked decrease in people standing around with nothing to do. And crime was down.

It wasn't hard to see where the money was going. The elimination of tariffs was a boon to small business, and the vast majority of small business in Alodia is in the informal sector. Houses started getting fixed up. Merchants started having a better selection of goods in better-outfitted market stalls. Imports of personal computers leaped by an astounding 800%, and four internet service providers opened up shop in 2001. (Previously, a single Aloville company had offered the only internet service in Alodia; its prices have since dropped by 50%.)

The Akuopha regime professes to have no inclination to regulate the surge in "underground" commerce, despite the fact that most analysts warn that an informal economic boom cannot go far toward rescuing a national economy — particularly one with whom the West refuses to deal.

Another success story in the Alodia regime's first year was the tourist trade, principally in its Atlantic resort city of Kahpri-Moloj. Taxes on hotels, restaurants, casinos and other entertainment services were removed, along with import duties. These had been (as they are across the developing world) a significant source of foreign exchange. With them removed, Alodian tourist attractions could compete very favorably. In addition, Alodia's traditional lack of restrictions on the "victimless crimes" of prostitution, gambling and recreational drugs have always leant Kahpri-Moloj an air of exoticism, making it a kind of "African Amsterdam." Marketing campaigns aimed at the wild side of Alodian nightlife found their mark among European and Japanese tourists. (And to provide a PR capstone to these developments, General Akuopha himself, a longtime amateur jazz musician, accepted an invitation to perform in a Kahpri-Moloj nightclub.)

While Alodia's economic reforms appear to be succeeding, their continued viability clearly depends on resolving the country's untenable political situation. Akuopha and his advisors know that Alodia's economy, however innovative, cannot hope to survive for long as a Cuba-style outcast. The regime has taken pains to call itself an "interim government" and has stated its intention to propose a new Constitution and to hold elections. The pressure is now on Akuopha to keep his promises. For his part, he refuses to accept the title of "President" (his official title remains unclear, but some fans have dubbed him "Tonton"), and has stated that he will not run for the office. Simon Abiama, a young lawyer and former aide to the deposed President Oshodi, appears to be Akuopha's anointed successor.

The political danger for Akuopha's regime has become increasingly clear-cut, and a showdown is coming. The influence of the Army in all that has happened in 2001 has been everywhere evident. Alodia's soldiers are well-paid — astoundingly, Alodian soldiers, even those with HIV/AIDS, are given full medical insurance and have access to medicines that other Alodians cannot hope to afford. Not surprisingly, their loyalty to General Akuopha and to the Army chain of command is, by all accounts, very strong. But, in the long term, Alodia's progressive economic climate is not compatible with a military dictatorship, and many Army personnel — particularly many well-paid and well-connected members of the Officer Corps — will be forced to seek employment in the civilian economy. Alodia's soldiers, like so many of today's workers, will have to face the rigors of downsizing. Should the army divide into hostile factions — as seems only too likely — it is far from clear that any organization, group or process in Alodia will be able to withstand the pressure.

Letter to the Editor

The Political Economist's story was remarkably evenhanded, although it retained the standard Western anti-Akuopha line. Certainly no one thinks that Alodia is the best of all possible worlds. Yet it remains true that even amid the graft-riddled "socialist" regimes of the 80s, Alodia's army was the best-equipped and most coherent in sub-Saharan Africa. Many attribute this phenomenon to the zealous and visionary leadership of Akuopha himself; others note less pure influences, such as persistent rumors of Mafia-like drug dealing. Nevertheless, Alodia's Army could be counted on, and that really made Akuopha's audacious reform plan achievable — so far, anyway.

Another fact that has, to my knowledge, never been reported anywhere, is the education program that the Alodian Army undertook during a hazily-defined period in the 1990s. It is said that a short course in funamental political economy, reading the works of Henry George, was instituted as part of basic military training, and for many years, every Alodian soldier has sat this course. If that is so (and it seems to be borne out by the Army's remarkably efficient assistance in the land cadastre initiative), then it represents a remarkable achievement. It also indicates that this "impetuous coup" has been actively planned for over a decade.

—Dan A. Sullivary, President, International Single Tax League

SOLDIERS BUST UP KAHPRI-MOLOJ CLUB RAMPAGE WOUNDS MANY – REASONS UNCLEAR

May 4, 2001. Last Saturday evening the celebrated Modu Quintet was performing at Tropicarctica, the Kahpri-Moloj nightclub, when for no apparent reason a riot began, instigated by a dozen Alodian Army regulars who were visibly drunk and belligerant according to many observers. The melee apparently broke out when two of the soldiers began to loudly berate the musical skills of the ensemble. When the two were asked to leave their buddies began knocking heads. At least ten people were injured and the Army had been presented a sizeable bill for damages to the club.

AKUOPHA'S EMERGENCY FUNDS

July 10, 2001, Now press is saying we should be worried, that General Sam has spent the treasury dry and soon the soldiers will not get their paychecks. But the Army will not run out of money anytime soon. Why? Because it has more than "land rent" in its pockets. Alodia is a poor country. Economists said that with no government revenue and no international financing we would not last this long! What did these funds come from,

> *Starting in mid-year 2001, a group of anti-Akuopha newspapers started to appear in Aloville, Gancha and Kahpri-Moloj. These were widely rumored to have been funded by landowning interests and multinational corporations. The first and best-known of these was* The Blade, *out of Aloville. Its rather chilling logo incorporated photos of traditional throwing knives, and the "vision eye" of Alodia's flag.*

that we had saved up for a rainy day? Who knew about this money?

Illicit drugs can be easily grown in hidden valleys, and the Army controls the roads and ports. Can there be any doubt that this is the answer to the mystery of Akuopha's "emergency funds"? And we know — do we not — how the USA responds to Dictators who send crack cocaine to afflict the children of New York and Seattle?

ALOVILLE FIREMEN IN NEW YORK!?!?

September 15, 2001, We sympathize with the good people of New York in the aftermath of the brutal attack on their city. But we ask you! Does the richest city in the richest country of the world need a team of two dozen firefighters, flown there on the tab of the cash-strapped Republic of Alodia? The actions of Akuopha's "Interim Government" get more and more irrational. This was nothing but a photo op! Did you catch the sight of our man standing atop with rubble with President Bush — and looking straight at the camera! Whether this fellow gets his hands dirty or not, no doubt "Tonton" will give him a bonus when he gets home.

AKUOPHA TICKLES THE IVORIES

March 30, 2002. It is not known whether ivory from African elephants forms the keys on the grand piano at the *Berceau de Chat*, Kahpri-Moloj's famed den of debauchery — but the head of Alodia's "Interim Government" will find out soon enough. General Akuopha has not seen fit even to name a title for the stool on which he has sat for fifteen months and shows no inclination to leave. Could this be because his mind is too full of music to care? He has announced he will play a gig at the *Berceau de Chat*, along with US chanteuse Andrea King and other luminaries, and he is practicing, some say as much as four hours daily.

No news from his sham of a "Constitutional Convention," no accounting for all of the so-called "land rent" grabbed from the people. Akuopha is too busy. He did have time in his busy schedule, however, to visit the cynical and irrelevant African Greens Summit — in Dakar, another town known for its music, women and high life. General Akuopha's position — whatever it is called — is nice work, if you can get it.

Over drinks, February 2002

The end-of-day "over cocktail" briefings have, by now, acquired a semi-official character. They function as a daily meeting of senior staff. Yet, they maintain their informality. Monique Sassafras, a newcomer to these meetings, has yet to begin to feel comfortable, although she has proven her importance to the team with her perceptive and timely understanding of popular trends. The Security Chief, nicknamed "Spook," a longtime associate of Akuopha's, has little to say on matters of policy, but is always well-attuned to political nuance.

SASSAFRAS: It is obvious that we will have to restrict immigation. It's just a matter of time.

BEHELE: I agree with you, don't get excited. I just said that Akuopha probably won't.

SASSAFRAS: *(ironic laugh)* Yes. We allow all the objects that anyone wants to bring past the borders, but no people.

ABIAMA: We didn't make the world.

SPOOK: *(entering the room)* Well why haven't you, Simon, my boy? What's the hold-up?

SASSAFRAS: No, we didn't make the world, but that's just what the World Bank says, we must face hard reality. Up to now we have acted like idealists. The migrants have family here.

ABIAMA: Then we'll let family in.

SASSAFRAS: Simon, where did you go to college? Suddenly, they'll all have family —

BEHELE: Ms. Sassafras, as you know well —

SASSAFRAS: I know only that —

BEHELE: The General puts up with quite a bit from

you, but your style fails to impress him. I suggest you and I confer, outside this room, and put together an argument. Does this seem wise to you?

SASSAFRAS: It does.

BEHELE: So. How does he sound on the piano?

SPOOK: Not bad. Really, I would say, perfectly passable for one whose hands have been hardened by decades of the unspeakable. If he sticks to the standards and leaves Andrea King in the limelight, he will acquit himself well for the photographers. But, of course, the album won't sell, because of punitive tariffs.

SIMON: We'll post it on the internet. Listen, why — still — does no one from the Constitutional team attend these meetings?

BEHELE: Because these meetings are unofficial —

SASSAFRAS: And deniable.

BEHELE: Quite right. And theirs are so public that the mind goes numb. I have no interest, really I don't. Let them debate, and then bring me the summary.

SPOOK: The General himself, Simon, has banned the Constitutional team, from our tete-a-tete. And you may have noticed that none of us has been called in to testify.

SIMON: And why is that?

SASSAFRAS: (clapping her hands) Simon! You will make such a good President one day. The Constitution is already written, is it not?

SPOOK: Ms. Sassafras, let me buy you a drink. I have not seen the final draft, but I suspect that the document will pass muster even in your market. (Akuopha enters) Sam! How are the fingers?

AKUOPHA: (holds up his hands, and looks at them, with a sigh) Weak, I'd say — but not paralyzed. Tell me about micro-credit in Aloville, and tell me how the black flies will be eradicated — and give me a scotch.

Alodia Swings

***People Magazine.* 11 May 2002.**

When was the last time you had the chance to dig an evening of jazz played by a Head of State? It doesn't happen often — and to the star-studded crowd that gathered this month, at the chic-y *Berceau de Chat* in Kahpri-Moloj, Alodia, it was a experience not to be missed.

The lineup on *Berceau de Chat* bandstand was historic. On bass, there was Ron Carter, from Miles Davis's 1960s quintet. On saxophone was George Coleman, another iconic Davis veteran. Alodian favorite son Papa Meissa Dieng was on drums. On vocals, Grammy winner Andrea King seemed to share a special accompanist/chanteuse rapport with her pianist: none other than 67-year old General Samuel Akuopha, for over a year the leader of Alodia's audacious new "land government."

The band played for ten evenings to a standing-room-only house, to jazz fans and Akuopha supporters — and while they did, the ramshackle streets of this West African resort town looked like the boulevards of Hollywood. An astouding who's who of stars turned out, from Muhammad Ali, Robert Redford and Susan Sarandon to rockers Bob Geldof and Bonnie Raitt and former US Senator Ronald Dellums. The music was — according to knowledgeable listener Dellums, "nicely crafted. Not too adventurous. A nice mix of standards, old songs that Andrea King handled very coolly, and General Akuopha showed a strong sense of swing. He's been rehearsing."

The political significance of the event, however, overshadowed the music. In January, 2001, Akuopha bemused the world when he seized power, insisting that "our ground must be cultivated with the conditions of economic justice and prosperity that makes it possible for democracy to take root." Akuopha's regime announced an immediate, unilateral default on Alodia's foreign debt. Pundits dismissied the regime as a lark, giving it little chance of surviving its first few months. But, over a year later, Akuopha's government has announced public programs to rebuild roads and eradicate insect pests, convened a constitutional convention and garnered considerable support from the Alodian peasantry.

Economic conditions in Alodia have surprised many. This year, some 30% of the seasonal workers who migrate from neighboring Burkina Faso to work in Alodian cocoa fields have not returned home after the harvest. Jobs in the cocoa plantations were scarce, because of trade sanctions imposed after Alodia's default. But, many construction and service jobs opened up in Kahpri-Moloj and the Capital city of Aloville.

Meanwhile, opposition press in Alodia has bitterly denounced Akuopha for allowing himself a jazz vacation (he is rumored to have been practicing daily for months), while his nation struggles with the full menu of problems facing Sub-Saharan Africa: poverty, crumbling infrastructure, AIDS and ecological havoc. But Akuopha and his aides do not seem to care about the bad press. Indeed, the General announced at the very beginning of his regime that the press would be absolutely free in Alodia — and so far he has been true to his word.

Akuopha with Andrea King at the *Berceau de Chat*

Students of West African (and jazz) history may recall that this is not the first time an Alodian Head of State has performed jazz in public. Jean-Henri Alo, Alodia's beloved leader and first President upon independence from France in 1961, was an avid jazz fan and musician. Alo played the saxophone; he and his friend Samuel Akuopha played together often in the late 50s. Under Alo's leadership, the new nation (then called Limbotho) issued postage stamps depicting jazz greats Miles Davis and John Coltrane. Unfortunately, however, although Blue Note Records was on hand to record this date, Jean-Henri Alo never appeared on record.

Ivorian Crisis Boosts Alodia

***Africa Report,* February 14 2003.** Since the Ivorian crisis began some five months ago, Alodia, like some other neighbouring countries, has received some bad and good effects. Many of Alodian nationals of the Djula ethnic group who managed to flee to Alodia have sworn not to return back to Cote D'Ivoire even if the war ceases today.

Most Djula, who are skillful traders, have since started their usual trade in Alodia.

Most neighbouring countries are now turning to Alodia to purchase those consumer items they once imported from Cote D'Ivoire.

A whopping sum of about a million people, including refugees of other ethnic groups, have now decided to resettle in Alodia.

To: Hiram Behele and Monique Sassafras
March 10, 2002
From: Samuel Akuopha
Re: Immigration Policy

Thank you both, for your well-reasoned recommendations.

Despite all the dangers of instability that you point out, we will not impose new immigration restrictions now.

You are correct that Alodia does already have immigration restrictions, but you neglect to observe that there is no agency with any staff, budget or mandate to enforce them; that is simply because, for decades, no significant numbers of people have wanted to move here. The cacao migrants were as regular as the seasons, but never before have they cared to stay.

Should we post uniformed soldiers at the borders to toss them out? Certainly, we could do that, although it would divert resources from other aims. But it would be unseemly. It would not jibe with our statements about human rights. As (and if) things begin to improve here, more people will want to come, yes. And we will have room for them, until an elected legislature decides to act otherwise.

Thank you again for all your irreplaceable service to our nation on its new path.

Proposed Constitution for the Republic of Alodia

***The Alodian Evening*. 1 September 2002**. *The commission has proposed its draft: over 13,000 words; longer than Nigeria's. Will anyone read it? The voters will decide, but at least they will have a choice. Here is the Constitution proposed by the interim government. It is less than one-sixth the length of the Commission's proposal, and it is not difficult to follow. Whether or not the Alodian people choose it, we shall eagerly cede power to a duly elected government. — Samuel Akuopha*

First Section - Bill of Rights

1. There shall be no national religion. All people shall freely exercise their religious beliefs. There shall be no abridgement of the freedom of speech, or of the press; or the right of the people peaceably to assemble, and to petition the government for a redress of grievances.

2. The right of the people to be secure against unreasonable searches and seizures, in their persons, houses, papers, and effects, shall not be violated. No searches shall be conducted, unless authorized by a duly issued warrant, based upon probable cause, supported by oath or affirmation, clearly and particularly describing the place to be searched, and the persons or things to be seized.

3. No person shall be held to answer for a felony, unless indicted by a grand jury. No person shall be tried more than once for the same offense, nor shall be compelled in any criminal case to be a witness against himself, nor be deprived of liberty or property without due process of law.

4. In all criminal prosecutions, the accused shall enjoy the right to a speedy and public trial, by an impartial jury of the district wherein the crime shall have been committed, which district shall have been previously ascertained by law, and to be informed of the nature and cause of the accusation; to be confronted with the witnesses against him; to have compulsory process for obtaining witnesses in his favor, and to have the assistance of counsel for his defense.

5. Cruel and unusual punishments shall not be inflicted, and no person's life shall be taken as punishment for any crime.

6. The right of ownership of material goods created and services performed, or goods and services lawfully exchanged, shall not be violated by taxation, confiscation or any other means. No tax shall be imposed on the production of material wealth, the provision of services or the sale or transport of goods.

7. Access to the bounty of nature, not created by human beings, being necessary to all life, the people's right to equal access to and enjoyment of the land and natural resources shall be secured. No persons or corporations holding title to land shall be deprived of such land without due process of law, but the rental value of all lands and natural opportunities shall be paid to the community. Land and resource values shall be assessed and collected in a manner prescribed by law. Assessment data shall be updated annually and made public, and landholders shall have the right to appeal their assessments in a court of law.

8. No lawful property shall be taken for public use without just compensation. The rental value of land and natural opportunities, being the rightful property of the community, shall not be construed as the property of any individual or group, and the public collection of such rental value shall not entitle the resource holder to compensation.

9. The enumeration in the Constitution of certain rights does not deny or disparage others retained by the people. The powers

not delegated to the Nation by the Constitution are reserved to the local governing bodies, or to the people.

10. Legislative, executive and judicial powers are vested in the National government and the local governing bodies. Powers not specifically delegated to the national government or to the several states are reserved to the local governing bodies, or to the people.

Second Section - Citizenship

1. All persons born in the territory of the State of Alodia are citizens of the Nation of Alodia. Other residents may become naturalized as citizens, in a manner that shall be prescribed by law.

2. Citizens having reached the age of at least twelve years shall be entitled to vote in all State and Local elections.

Third Section - Legislature

1. All legislative powers shall be vested in a Congress of Alodia, which shall be composed of a House of Representatives and a Regional Council.

2. The House of Representatives shall be composed of one hundred members, who are citizens of the Nation of Alodia, and shall be elected by a direct popular vote in the following manner:

The initial election shall be held no longer than six months after the adoption of this Constitution as set forth in the seventh section. In the initial election, the one hundred candidates who receive the greatest number of votes shall be elected. After one year, the twenty-five representatives who received the lowest numbers of votes shall end their term, and twenty-five representatives shall be elected by direct popular vote. After two years, the twenty-five representatives who received the next-lowest numbers of votes in the initial election shall end their term and twenty-five representatives shall similarly be elected.

In the third year the twenty-five representatives who received the next-lowest numbers of votes in the initial election shall end their term and twenty-five representatives shall similarly be elected. In the fourth year the remaining twenty-five representatives shall end their terms and twenty-five representatives shall similarly be elected. After the fourth year, all representatives shall serve terms of four years.

3. The Regional Council shall be composed of three members from each regional division, or state, which shall be elected by a direct popular vote within that regional division. No person shall be elected to the regional Council unless he or she is a resident of the state represented, and a citizen of the Nation of Alodia. Members of the Regional Council shall be elected in the following manner.

The initial election shall be held no longer than six months after the adoption of this Constitution as set forth in the seventh section. In the initial election, each state shall elect three members to the council. After two years, members who received the lowest number of votes in the initial election in that state shall end their terms, and each state shall elect one member. In the fourth year, members who received the second-lowest number of votes in the initial election in that state shall end their terms and each state shall elect one member. In the sixth year the remaining members shall end their terms and each state shall elect one member. After the sixth year, all council members shall serve terms of six years.

All costs of elections to the Regional Council shall be paid by the local governing bodies, in proportion to the aggregate land rent contained therein, as determined under section 4,5.

4. Vacancies in the House of Representatives shall be filled by direct popular election of all voters; vacancies in the Regional Council shall be filled by direct popular election within the state concerned; the timetable for such elections shall be prescribed by law.

5. No person shall be elected to either house of the Legislature if the cumulative amount spent on his or her election campaign, by the candidate or by any organization seeking to aid his or her candidacy, is more than twelve times the mean salary of a wage-earning full-time working citizen during the year immediately preceding the election in question.

6. This Constitution is the Supreme Law of the Nation of Alodia. In recognition that events influenced by history, technological change, and cultural interaction cannot be fully foreseen, the Legislature shall enact such laws as secure the rights set forth in this Constitution.

7. The Legislature shall submit an annual budget for the Nation of Alodia which, upon approval of the Executive, shall become Law. National expenditures may not exceed the total assessed Rent of natural opportunities in the current year. Each budget shall include such resources as are requested by the Executive, and approved by the Legislature, to be necessary to secure the current assessments as described in section 4,5.

8. Measures passed by a majority of both houses of the Legislature shall be submitted to the Executive for approval. If that approval is denied within two weeks' time, the measure in question shall become Law if it is approved in two weeks' time by two thirds of both houses of the Legislature.

Fourth Section - Executive

1. Executive powers shall be vested in the President of the Nation of Alodia. The President shall be elected every four years by direct popular vote. A Vice President shall be elected at the same time, for the same term. Should the President die, the Vice President shall assume the office of President.

2. No persons shall be elected to the offices of President and Vice President if the cumulative amount spent on their election campaign, by the candidates or by any organization seeking to aid their candidacy, is more than twenty-five times the mean

salary of a wage-earning full-time working citizen during the year immediately preceding the election in question.

3. The President shall be commander in chief of the Armed Forces of Alodia. He shall have power, with the advice and consent of the Regional Council, to make treaties, provided a majority of the Regional Council concur; and he shall nominate, and with the advice and consent of the Regional Council, shall appoint ambassadors, other public ministers and consuls, judges of the Supreme Court, and all other officers of the Nation, whose appointments are not herein otherwise provided for, and which shall be established by law: but the legislature may by law vest the appointment of such inferior officers, as they think proper, in the President alone, in the courts of law, or in the heads of departments.

4. The President shall receive ambassadors and other public ministers; he shall take care that the laws be faithfully executed, and shall commission all the officers of the Nation.

5. The President shall deliver to the Legislature, and simultaneously make public, by the first day of each year, a full, current assessment of the rental value of all land and national opportunities within the Nation of Alodia.

6. The President, Vice President and all civil officers of the Nation, shall be removed from office on impeachment for, and conviction of, treason, bribery, or other high crimes, or gross incapacitation. No officer shall be impeached except upon a two-thirds vote of both Houses.

Fifth Section - Judicial

1. The judicial power of the Nation of Alodia shall be vested in one Supreme Court, and in such inferior courts as the Legislature may from time to time ordain and establish. The Supreme Court shall consist of nine Justices. Justices shall be nominated by the President and approved by a majority vote of both houses of the Legislature. Their terms shall be for life, subject to impeachment as set forth in Section 4,6.

Sixth Section - Amendments

1. Amendments to this Constitution shall be proposed by a two-thirds vote of both Houses of the Legislature, and approved by a direct popular vote on the question of Amendment, said amendment having been widely and clearly publicized for a period of at least six months.

Seventh Section - Ratification

1. This Constitution shall be presented to the people of Alodia and made universally available. If it is approved by a majority in a direct popular vote, held at least six months after the draft Constitution is made available to the public, it shall be adopted as the Constitution of the Nation of Alodia.

Alodia Catches Up with River Blindness

The Political Economist. September 2002

During the 1990s, most of West Africa fought a largely successful battle against onchocerciasis, or River Blindness, and the black fly whose bite causes the disease. With the aid of the United Nations and a number of NGOs, including the Carter Center, many fertile areas that had been rendered uninhabitable for decades were re-opened to homesteading. Although there were all manner of legal and infrastructural obstacles to the resettlement in many nations, the potential for increased agricultural production is still enormous, and the fight against river blindness remains, if not an unqualified success, then certainly a bright spot in an otherwise dismal African decade.

Alodia, unfortunately, lagged behind her neighbors in this regard. There was, indeed, a considerable effort to eliminate the foggy clouds of black flies that appeared all around Lake Banneker after the rainy season, but it was concentrated around the Southern and Eastern parts of the lake, around the capital city of Aloville, and other areas that were associated with the mining of the gem aichacite. Essentially, the program succeeded in driving the flies to the northern part of the lake, where they were allowed to afflict and to drive out what few peasants remained. The Northwestern shore of Lake Banneker had been sparsely settled ever since the flooding, caused in the 1960s by the Alo Dam, that wiped out many villages along the Jasil River.

However, those lands in the Nosenada Province, in the northern half of Lake Banneker, are among the most fertile in the country. The main obstacle is the black fly. Without competition from humans and their pesticides (and having been driven from its other habitats in the 1990s campaigns), the prodigious little bug remains a formidable foe in Nosenada. A sustained campaign of spraying shorelines and rivers is needed. Recently, the interim government of Samuel Akuopha has announced that it will undertake such a program. This policy was likely influenced by lobbying from the outspoken Dr. Cleopatra Paulin of *Medicins Sans Frontiers,* who, in an extraordinary televised interview with Akuopha last April, challenged him to demonstrate his commitment to land reform by eliminating the black flies. At the time, Akuopha demurred, arguing that the restructuring of Alodia's tax system was more important.

A year later, however, it appears that the "interim government" has a few Francs in its coffers, and that Paulin's advice has been taken to heart. In addition to the black fly eradication initiative, the government has promised to restore and maintain roads in and to the Nosenada province, provide regular bus transportation, and implement a micro-credit program for anyone willing to undertake a homestead in the area.

Submerged forests in Lake Banneker

Alodia: How Has the Regime Survived?

***Time*. 2 December 2002**

On New Year's Day, 2001, General Samuel Akuopha of Alodia announced a unilateral default on Alodia's foreign debt. International reactions were dismissive. Of course, WTO sanctions went into place immediately; as of January 2, 2001 there were no markets for Alodia's exports of cocoa and coffee. Full cargo ships sat in port, without destinations. Disbursements of loan and aid money were stopped. Alodia had to live on whatever cash it had on hand. No one thought this could last, and Akuopha's declaration was shrugged off as a stunt. The world's disbelief provided the regime with a critical buffer of time, during which it seems to have managed to explain what was happening to key business figures.

Akuopha knew that Alodia had little independent business community outside of those with intimate connections to the government. Not all of those people supported him, but many did — military coups are a fairly common feature in African politics, and the new leader's standing with the "business community" was a function of how firmly he controlled the army. Akuopha's "odd notions" about land and taxation were not a major consideration for them. The public detractors of Aukopha's regime either came from the small community of independent business people (many involved with transnational corporations, particularly on the cocoa plantations) and infiltrators from abroad. These were "consultants" or NGO officials, mostly from the United States, and their subsequent activities revealed many of them to have been tasked with undermining the independent regime. However, they seemed to lack an effective strategy for this. Their efforts, in any case, were curiously understated compared to those of similar agents in countries like Cameroon, or Angola.

However, there was a crucial period — really, all of 2001 — during which the Alodian government appeared to have no sources of revenue. Nothing could have happened without clandestine sources of interim financing. What were these? Widespread rumor held that a large drug-smuggling operation had been operated by secret army units. Though no hard proof came to light, it seems likely that this was the case. In any case, having gained some time from the world's initial disbelief, the regime got much-needed early relief by securing a trade deal with China. Now there was foreign exchange coming in (perhaps not so very much, but at least it established a plausible source for hard currency).

The China trade deal roughly coincided with the beginning of the Army's land cadastre campaign — yet another seemingly outrageous step. Pundits around the world dubbed it "Akuopha's stroll in the countryside" and lambasted the foolhardy plan to "regularize a whole country's real estate market in one fell swoop." The media were virtually unanimous in their judgment that Akuopha's plan could not possibly succeed. This turned out to be the most important reason for the West's lack of interference: Akuopha's stunt, as they saw it, would inevitably fade away. There was just no way it could work.

Indeed, the campaign could not have succeeded without the knowledgeable work of thousands of Alodian soldiers — a phenomenon that was widely documented by an incredulous press. The soldiers went about, in advance of the American assessment team, explaining that no one's property would be confiscated; their mission was to determine what pieces of land belonged to which people. This was determined, for the most part, by the "walk until the dogs start barking" method — in other words, the word of peasants was respected, and when there was conflict, traditional village elders were called in. The soldiers were placed in areas where their ethnic backgrounds matched those of the locals — and the whole process went through with surprisingly little conflict.

Once tenure was established, the cadastre team could use maps to determine land value. In practice, the process was more difficult in cities, despite the fact that land ownership records did exist there. Land ownership in Aloville, as in many third-world cities, was a maze of intricate conflicts and counter-claims. These would certainly have taken years to resolve, had not the program of collecting the full economic rent smoked out speculative title-holders. In the end, land titles in Aloville and Kahpri-Moloj tended to go to those who were prepared to develop sites, whether or not they originally had the most legitimate claim to title.

All of these processes were just getting underway in Alodia when the events of September 11, 2001 changed our world, igniting the "global war on terror." Oddly, Alodia was probably the only country in the world that benefitted from the events of September 11, 2001. The distraction could not have come at a better time for Akuopha. Alodia immediately sent a dozen Aloville firefighters to the wreckage at Ground Zero, one of whom was famously photographed at Gound Zero with George W. Bush. No other African nation did anything of the sort, and the photo-op focused a wave of coverage on Alodia's experiment — which was now less dismissive. The Bush Administration's invasion of Afghanistan, and its obsession with Saddam Hussein, seemed to let Alodia slip beneath its radar. (Alodia did have a large Muslim region in the north. One of its leading Imams issued a statement early on, disavowing Al Quaeda and terrorism. This probably had some carrot-and-stick motivation from Akuopha and the army — but, in any case, there were no reports of Islamic extremism in Alodia.)

Akuopha declared early on that he would not be a dictator for long, and that nothing he began would stay in place without the validation of Alodia's voters. Ironically, this declaration was reassuring to Western interests. Having thus far failed to stop Akuopha's unlikely success, they thought sure they would have him cornered when it came time for a constitutional referendum. A national policy as simple and transparent as "collection of land rent for public revenue" could hardly be expected to survive the onslaught of a panel of constitutional commissioners who represented all the country's economic players. The commission would create a huge, impenetrable document, and thereby tie up the issue of land rent in a legalistic maze — exactly as Nigeria had done. They were on the verge of accomplishing this, when the commission's draft constitution faced an unexpected last-minute competitor. The very week that the commission's work was to be made public, Akuopha issued a remarkably short, readable document, strikingly similar to the original United States constitution — except that its Bill of Rights came first. Furthermore, the Akuopha team's draft constitution abolished government at the state level (a nation of some 25 million people, Alodia had been comprised of eleven states). This ostensibly radical step was much to the liking of ordinary Alodians, particularly in rural areas, who had long been impatient with corrupt state bureaucracies.

The new constitution was a runaway winner. Now, however, begins the hard process of making Alodia's radical plan work in daily life. Alodia's experiment has survived far more than anyone thought possible. Next, Alodians will be called, under the new constitution, to elect a brand-new government. After that, Alodia's radical new rent-as-revenue system — so promising in theory — will face the test of real-world politics.

Immigration: We Must Take Our Medicine

The Alodian Evening, 15 June 2003

One of the most important questions to be faced by the new administration of Simon Abiama how Alodia will handle the huge influx of people who suddenly want to settle here. Samuel Akuopha resisted all the calls to set a policy "before it was too late." By refusing to compromise in the short term, he kept his open-borders ideology on the table. But now, Alodia's government has to govern.

A few thousand migrant workers from Burkina Faso and Mali have traditionally come into Alodia each year for seasonal work in the cocoa and coffee fields. Because of the effects of trade sanctions in 2000-01, the workers found little harvesting to do when they arrived. However, word came to them of construction and other work in the cities, particular in the Kahpri-Moloj tourist industry. So, most of them stayed in Alodia, and rather than returning home, many sent for their families to join them.

Until this year, Alodia was fortunate not to have to face an influx of political refugees. The Ivorian crisis has brought tens of thousands of people into the country. Foprtunately, though, our neighbors, Ghana, Cote d'Ivoire, Burkina Faso and Mali, remained politically stable. However, as economic conditions continued to improve, an influx of workers would eventually make it hard to sustain the wage increases and new public works that we have recently enjoyed. Alodia's population has already increased by 9% over pre-coup levels. Most of the increase was due to immigration — and this led to a slight, but consistent, decline in the propulation growth rate of Alodia's neighbors.

This has raised complaints, because the people moving into Alodia have tended to be highly productive adults.

The best thing that could happen to Alodia, in this regard, would be if its neighbors were to adopt the same set of reforms. Alodia hopes to be the first in a line of happy African dominoes. If other nations don't fall in line, however, it is hard to see how one small nation, however prosperous, could prop up its entire region. Abiama must move to restrict immigration.

President-elect Simon Abiama

Beneath the Uniform: Samuel Akuopha

Rolling Stone. **21 October 2003**

On the day after New Year's, 2001, a historic political speech was broadcast, in mid-afternoon, on local television in Aloville, Alodia. Relatively few people heard the speech; relatively few people in that West African country had access to television — or to electricity, for that matter — at the time. In that speech, General Samuel Akuopha announced that Alodia's Government had been unseated, its constitution suspended, and — this was the part that people noticed — it would immediately default on its foreign debt.

The coup, and subsequent land and taxation reforms established by Akuopha's "interim government," were widely dismissed and ridiculed. No one thought they could possibly last. Yet they have — until now, at any rate. This May, Akuopha stepped down in favor of his duly-elected successor, Simon Abiama. Akuopha has stated his intention to retire from public life to play his piano. He was the leader of what was by most accounts, Africa's most audaciously successful revolution, dubbed "Tonton" (Uncle) and nearly sanctified by his grateful people. Yet even now, little is known about him.

The demeanor of Samuel Akuopha was not the sort one would expect from an African dictator. He was long known as an extremely private person, and outside of the staunchly loyal Alodian army, few even knew of him at all. During the two decades prior to his being catapulted to international fame, his name had appeared precisely once in the *New York Times.*

Akuopha has declined all requests for interviews, after the Alodian Constitution was adopted, and the recent Presidential election got underway. What we have been able to piece together of his life story is singular and, in many ways, rather poignant. He was a very close friend, ideological *confrere* and musical collaborator with Alodia's founding hero, Jean-Henri Alo. Both attended university and sowed their wild oats in the Parisian jazz scene of the 1950s. Perhaps incongruously, they were both caught up in individualist, libertarian philosophy — a tendency which would significantly affect the subsequent history of Alodia. But Akuopha's real passion — which he shared with Alo — was jazz music. Both were itinerant players in Paris clubs (Alo played the tenor saxophone), and they spent much of their time with other musicians and hangers-on in the scene, practicing and jamming. Akuopha met his wife, Yamina, there — a beautiful, rather mysterious Algerian woman who was a sometime jazz singer, and very much part of the scene. Like many, she dabbled with drugs, and eventually became addicted to heroin, although Akuopha may not have been aware of the extent of her habit for some time. As Alo and Akuopha began making more frequent trips back and forth between Limbotho and France, Samuel and Yamina saw less of each other. Though he apparently greatly missed both his wife and his musical career, he felt that his duty to the new nation could not be refused. Yamina, born in Algeria and raised in France, had never been to West Africa and resisted his requests that she move there. She died under mysterious circumstances in 1961, soon after the Republic of Limbotho gained its independence.

His wife's death was a tremendous blow to Akuopha, and it

had much to do with the two traits for which he became known over the years — his quiet, retiring manner, and his insistence on rigorous discipline. Indeed, it is thought that this is why he initially volunteered for the task of organizing Limbotho's military. This is the view of an Alodian official, a longtime Akuopha associate, who would not reveal his name because of a continuing role in Simon Abiama's administration. "He wanted to immerse himself in a thoroughly ordered existence — and perhaps, if need be, face danger in battle. He said as much to me, sometimes. In certain moods."

When Jean-Henri Alo died in 1964, Samuel Akuopha had become firmly established in his role of commander of the Limbothan (soon to become Alodian) army. "Now, he had lost both his wife and his best friend," the associate recalls. "Returning to Paris was not an option. His only friend was his work, and he threw himself into it zealously."

It has been called an accident of history that Alodia's unusually efficient and well-trained army was never called to war. In the nation's early years, its "libertarian" politics were embraced by the United States as an alternative to socialist-oriented African liberation movements. (In its early years Alodia attracted a thriving tourist industry with its notably low taxes, and even to this day it has refused to criminalize "victimless" activities such as prostitution and drug possession.) Yet the army's long reputation for efficiency and high morale must also have been a factor. Alodia may have gone through booms and busts, and wild swings in political orientation, but it was never threatened with attack. Evidently this peculiar — and fortunate — aspect of Alodia's history had much to do with the personal history and obsessions of Samuel Akuopha.

The coup that Akuopha commanded in 2001 was not a precipitous thing; indeed, seems to have been planned in intricate detail for perhaps as long as a decade. Sometime in the 1990s, Akuopha and his Generals instituted, of all things, a required course in "Fundamental Economics" as part of the basic training of every Alodian soldier. This, at least, is no secret; although it was not discussed before 2001, as far as can be found now, it was fully integrated into military routine, and many people have since reported on it. "Probably it was considered a whim of the General's," said Major Ali Guindo, who has served in the Alodian army since 1989. "It was such a habitual thing. Nobody questioned it — recruits reported for their economics course, where they read *Progress and Poverty* by Henry George. I think many of the men thought it was silly at first, but they ended up liking the studies." It was a remarkable initiative. The team of land assessors hired by the regime in 2001-02 were astonished at the level of economic understanding displayed by regular soldiers, told off to escort them around the countryside. This fact, more than any other, demonstrates the meticulous planning that went into Alodia's coup.

As he became world-famous, Akuopha tried to remove himself from the limelight. The accusations of megalomania surrounding his famous Kahpri-Moloj jazz gig were spectacularly off the mark. Akuopha had not seriously practiced the piano for decades. But, the longer Alodia's "outrageous political stunt" defied the predictions of imminent collapse, the more assiduously reporters dug into Akuopha's story. It was only a matter of time before some reporter would unearth his musical past — and some impresario would invite him to perform. When the offer came to him, Akuopha set terms that he thought couldn't possibly be met: he demanded a cast of all-stars for his band. When all the performers agreed to come (save one, not an all-star but an old friend who, after so many years, could not be found), Akuopha was forced to keep his promise. Once he started practicing, of course, he fell in love with the music all over again. The success of Samuel Akuopha's triumphant return to the bandstand came as a great surprise to him. Akuopha played an engagement of ten nights at The *Berceau de Chat*, a rather chic-y club near the sea in Kahpri-Moloj. "He had not been that relaxed, that free, in many years,"

recalled the longtime associate.

As Alodia's economy struggled to reorient itself in 2001, it faced a "cash crisis." It was widely rumored that sales of illegal drugs — illegal in other countries, that is — carried on by top-secret elements of the army, provided an indispensable source of hard currency during this period (and indeed had been doing so for some time). This could not have gone on without Akuopha's knowledge — and reluctant approval. He felt haunted by the Faustian bargain he felt he had made to secure Alodia's transformation. Akuopha seems to have felt tainted by this past, which somehow rendered him unfit to take on the role that Alodians increasingly wanted him to play. His longtime associate recalls, "It was a grim business for him, he really seemed to believe that his own soul had to be lost, if the country was to be saved." As the audacious reforms took hold, the local economy actually began to prosper, and Alodia remained unfazed by Western sanctions (and unattacked by the United States), Samuel Akuopha became more and more of a local hero. His reticence in the face of this adulation served only to give his public image an air of statesmanlike reserve which increased his appeal. In fact, however, the more public attention (and TV invitations) Akuopha got, the more effort he put into launching the career of his suave and handsome heir-apparent, Simon Abiama.

Samuel Akuopha has showed up at Kahpri-Moloj's *Berceau de Chat* a few times since, with little fanfare, sitting in with whoever happened to be playing, a bit like Woody Allen's relationship with Michael's Pub in New York. "He will chat with people between sets," laughs his associate, "but he makes sure to bring enough security to allow him to slip away when he's ready to." *Tonton's Blues,* the live album of Akuopha's historic date at the Cat's Cradle, sold well enough that the release of another album on Blue Note Records has been announced for later this year.

Dare I hope for my native land?

For so long it has been about surviving, even those of us with
good cool water, with kids
in prep school football — it was only one sliver away from the
old friend wasting,
the brother begging, rush hour smoke belching mayhem,
motorcycle runs down child.

the good riverbank bloated, cancerous,
the good land abscessed,
the forests drowned, only the flies
prospering, for so long
it has been about getting above the wretched
mass, stepping on them if need be

My native land has barely
claimed a moment's thought in its addled head, for so long
busied with preserving what could be saved,
teaching who could stand to learn
We've only been weary, not sunk,
not lost, but weary with striving and frugality

Thank God at least we had no oil
The cocoa, the green stones, the slaves,
they were enough

Heia! cried Cesaire
for those who never invented, never explored, never tamed
yet without whom (trudging amid the lost, funky, trudging
throng)
the world would not be the world

Dare I hope for my native land
now being called to join the World on its own terms?
It's own terms? It's OWN? When has this
lovely, bright, open land (the green stones merely
  a distillation of its air in days maybe someone
  could remember) WHEN
has this so punished, so trammeled land
been in a position to name its terms?

Have we recourse to urbanity? Are we nattily suited? Are we
  in with the in crowd?

Did our good Tonton earn his stylish moment,
building his good foundation,
all those years, with stones?

I will watch the piled yams, the festivals and feasts,
and if the kids come to their classes well-fed, and alert
and if, in deciding what to build
they hearken more to the griot's tale
and yearn less for messages from outer space,
then I will dare to hope for my native land.

— **Annette-Rosa Mukeni, Aloville, May 1, 2003**

Epilogue: Could It Happen?

During the period when the Alodia story was first being told, I was a devoted fan of the TV series *The West Wing*. I saw Jed Bartlet and Samuel Akuopha somewhat as kindred spirits, as more-or-less credible fulfillments of progressive wishes. Of course, devotees of Samuel Akuopha's political philosophy saw President Bartlet as missing the point, squandering the greatest opportunity: a Nobel Prize-winning economist who didn't understand the land question! The story of Alodia, at any rate — in its modest, edge-of-the-headlines way, stayed true to the Georgist vision.

What is that vision, and why is it so important? Henry George's classic book *Progress and Poverty* (1879) explained the rationale for the economic remedy that came to be known as the "Single Tax." George made a number of important observations about the economic role of land (which, as an economic factor, includes all natural opportunities and resources — everything that exists, except for human beings and their products). He saw that land acquires a market value independently of anything its owner might do. Land becomes valuable as a community grows around it, and overall demand increases for the opportunities it embodies. Seeing this, landholders can hold land out of use, and then, when they are ready, collect an unearned payment for access to land's community-created value. Meanwhile, in order to pay for public goods and services, such as roads, schools, port facilities, police and fire protection, etc., communities impose taxes on society's producers — those who create goods and services. Such taxation penalizes the production of wealth and reduces effective demand for the products of labor. Yet the public services financed by taxation further increase the value of land — a rental value which landholders collect, having done nothing whatever to create it! This logic led Henry George to his "Single Tax" remedy: that the full value of land (land only, not buildings or other improvements) should be collected by the community for public revenue, and all other taxes (on sales, income, imports or any other form of commerce) should be abolished.

Although Samuel Akuopha's unilateral default on Alodia's foreign debt raised more hackles and got more press, this — the Single Tax remedy — was the heart of his program. Debt repudiation could not have been sustained, had this not been implemented successfully. Here is a partial list of its consequences:

— ***A shift from exports to production for domestic consumption.*** Trade sanctions imposed against Akuopha's debt repudiation virtually canceled all of Alodia's export markets at once. Large areas were devoted to producing palm oil or cacao beans, export crops whose market disappeared. Lots of farmland was diverted to growing food for local consumption. The GDP seemed to drop, but most people were better off, because a great deal of this food was traded and consumed outside of formal markets.

— ***Regularization of real estate ownership.*** A little-discussed result of Alodia's Land Cadastre program was that for the first time, hundreds of thousands of small holders were given clear legal title to the places where they lived and worked. The land rent, if any, would be collected by the government. However, people's buildings and improvements had now become assets which they could confidently improve, sell or borrow against. This was similar to the program advocated by Hernando de Soto in his book *The Mystery of Capital* — however, Alodia achieved those benefits without falling into the trap of legalizing land speculation and privatizing the unearned income of land rent.

— ***An urban building boom.*** Holders of real estate in Alodia's cities — particularly the resort town of Kahpri-Moloj — saw the writing on the wall very quickly: land values were, relatively, quite high in the cities. The government was threatening to tax those values away, yet impose no taxation whatever on new construction, or the commence that would happen there. The seasonal cocoa workers from Burkina Faso and Mali found little work on the cocoa plantations, but word quickly spread that there were construction jobs aplenty to be found in Aloville and Kahpri-Moloj.

— ***A decline in absentee landlordism.*** Foreign landowners in Alodia — as in many other developing countries — expected to hold large acreages at little or no cost. In return for providing employment opportunities (such as they were) they expected unfettered access to land. If Alodia insisted on charging rent for these lands, then cocoa and palm oil could be produced just as easily in neighboring countries, who did not impose such fees. Urban landholders, meanwhile, would be compelled either to build on their land or abandon it.

These were economic effects that every post-colonial country desired, of course — but which none of them could ever achieve under the burden of high foreign debt and their consequent dependence on export-oriented production, an unhealthy condition that has been called "economic bulimia." The only cure for that disease is to replace foreign demand with domestic demand — which is exactly what the Georgist remedy would do.

These economic effects of shifting to a rent-as-revenue policy are striking enough. But there may be an even more profound "rightness" to this program for a nation such as Alodia.

One motif that kept coming up in the Alodia story was the widespread support, and affectionate vote of confidence, afforded to Akuopha by the common people. Akuopha was espousing an economic theory unlike anything they had ever heard of, yet it seemed to resonate with them in comfortable ways. I think there is a good reason for this — that it is, in other words, an entirely plausible aspect of the story. Henry George wrote during the gilded age: the time when the social ills brought forth by industrialization were being most deeply and pervasively felt. He saw — as did Karl Marx — how the "laissez faire" model of monopoly capitalism was brutal, dehumanizing and self-defeating. He also saw, however, that private ownership and free economic competition were essential to a progressive modern economy. Civilization had to find a way to reconcile the eternal fact of the commons — the equal right of each person to use and share the gifts of nature — with the great productive power of a modern market economy. No other economic proposal even pretended to do that. The issue was defined out of existence. Land became either a hard asset for the "real estate industry" and the "FIRE sector" — or a romantic issue for do-gooder environmentalists.

Across the continent of Africa (as, in different ways, in the Americas as well), a "European" model of land tenure was imposed by imperial powers. This was sometimes accomplished by force, but more often it was done by fraud, as indigenous rulers were persuaded to sign contracts whose provisions they didn't understand — not because they were unable to understand them, but because the contracts were misrepresented. Many African societies had sophisticated production, trade networks and monetary systems before European contact. It would have been most interesting to see how things would have developed had European technology been allowed to mix organically, via processes of trade, with African economic institutions.

Meanwhile, there were many communities in West Africa that had been passed by, in some ways, by modern economics. People eked out a living as well as they could, and it mattered little whether production was "formal." As late as 2000, a well-known Nigerian news magazine was running a full-page ad that showed two panicky men carrying bags of money out of a burning house — urging Nigerians to consider the benefits of depositing their money in banks. Old tribal ideas regarding land tenure survived in some communities — often because those places had not yet become economically important enough for those ideas to be forced aside. In many places the old notions *were* forced aside — but recently enough for them to linger in many memories. People didn't pretend to know about "economics" — but they heard Akuopha saying that land was not to be bought and sold for the profit of unknown people from far away. That would have rung true to them. They might be skeptical about it ever happening, but they'd have no reason to oppose it.

Once again I find myself speaking from within the fiction of Alodia. I do so because I'm extremely fond of this story, and particularly of its reluctant hero, Akuopha. But I'm afraid I'll have to step out of the tale, back into the real world, to address the inevitable question, ***Could it happen?*** Not, would it work? — there is general agreement that such a program would indeed work, pretty much as this story lays it out, if only a country could be persuaded to begin it, and the global "powers that be" would allow it to proceed. No, the real question is, ***Could*** it happen? Could a sovereign nation in the real world, with things as they are, ever be persuaded to take such an outrageous step?

The reader will notice various "gods out of the box" in our tale. We relied on a military coup — not the vagaries of democratic process — to get the ball rolling. We found Alodia convenient (if unsavory) sources of interim funding; we even found a way to let the 9/11 attacks work in Alodia's favor. However, truth often shows itself to be stranger than fiction, and, arguably, none of these things is implausible enough to remove our tale from the realm of possibility.

However, I think there is one vital plot element in the Alodia story that makes it possible for us to answer, "Could it happen?" in the affirmative. It isn't something the press would dwell on; most readers will see it as an incidental detail; many Georgists, even, would miss its fundamental importance.

What is it? You'll recall that outside commentators, including the Georgist economist Mason Gwartemann who assisted the cadastral team, were surprised at how well-prepared the regular Alodian soldiers were for this work. The whole program could not have succeeded without the swift and effective compilation of a national land cadastre — a task which virtually every outside commentator declared to be impossible. Yet the Alodian soldiers went about this task efficiently — and knowledgeably — and got it done on time.

How was this possible? It later became known that for at

How was this possible? It later became known that for at least a decade, a course on basic economics using Henry George's *Progress and Poverty,* had been part of the basic training regimen for every Alodian soldier. The course had become part of the routine. The army maintained a staff of instructors; the ten-lesson course was an established element of the boot-camp regimen. It had been that way long enough that nobody bothered to question it; recruits were taught how to fire and service weapons, fix jeeps, shine boots, and fix the economy. This "education process" was slow, patient, incremental, and seemed to have no culminating objective in view. But, on General Akuopha's orders, they just kept doing it, over and over and over.

Thus, when the time came for Akuopha to make his move, he knew that there existed a critical mass of people in Alodia who *knew what he was talking about.* Without them, his audacious, quixotic coup wouldn't have lasted a month, just as all the Western pundits predicted.

That tells us that the truer question isn't "Could a sovereign nation ever be persuaded to adopt this program?" The real question is, "Could an educational program ever succeed in creating a critical mass of people who understand the fundamental importance of this idea?" Time will tell. In the meantime, I hope you've been delighted by the Alodia story, and are inspired to get to work on its real-world sequel.

Index

Fictional characters are disignated by an asterisk.

T

U

V

W

The Henry George Institute

is a nonprofit, membership organization dedicated to bringing the economic ideas of Henry George to the attention of the public.

Our main vehicle in this mission is the three-part series of distance-learning courses called ***Principles of Political Economy***, which is offered to students around the world both by regular mail and on the Internet. Our courses are offered tuition-free, with a small charge for materials and expenses.

Understanding Economics

(www.henrygeorge.org) This fundamental course is suitable for students without any prior training in economics, yet offers insights that can benefit professional economists. Using consistent definitions and logic, the course analyzes the great mysteries of political economy: why does poverty deepen as material progress improves? Why are there seemingly intractable boom/ bust cycles?

Applied Economics: Globalization and Trade

(www.truefreetrade.org) A timely course that uses the principles of Georgist political economy to decode the mysteries of today's "global economy." Can free trade ever benefit a country, or must it always protect its jobs and industries? Is development incompatible with environmental sustainability?

Economic Science

(www.politicaleconomy.org) The third course in our series offers a deeper examination of the natural laws of supply and demand, rent, production and distribution of wealth, and the role of money. Georgist political economy is compared with current neoclassical and Marxist interpretations.

Enroll today!

Made in the USA
Charleston, SC
06 December 2010